— THE —
TERRI LYNNE LOKOFF
CHILD
CARE
FOUNDATION

*A portion of the proceeds of this book
will be donated to*

The Terri Lynne Lokoff Child Care Foundation
*www.childcareabc.org * Phone: 610-992-1140*

THE PROGRESSION OF WEALTH

THE PROGRESSION OF WEALTH

Jay L. Heller, CPA, PFS
Brian Kohute, CPA, CFA

InforMedia
Plymouth Meeting, Pennsylvania
2003

This book includes information from many sources and gathered from many personal experiences. It is published for general reference and is not intended to be a substitute for independent verification by readers when necessary and appropriate. The book is sold with the understanding that neither the authors nor publisher is engaged in rendering any legal, psychological, or accounting advice. The publisher and authors disclaim any personal liability, directly or indirectly, for advice or information presented within. Although the authors and publisher have prepared this manuscript with utmost care and diligence and have made every effort to ensure the accuracy and completeness of the information contained within, we assume no responsibility for error, inaccuracies, omissions, or inconsistencies.

ISBN: 0-9744756-0-2

ATTENTION: QUANTITY DISCOUNTS ARE AVAILABLE TO YOUR COMPANY OR EDUCATIONAL INSTITUTION for reselling, educational purposes, subscription incentives, gifts, or fund raising campaigns.
Please contact us at 1 - 800 - 535 - 2623 or www.hjfinancialgroup.com.

Securities and Investment Advisory Services offered through
Capital Analysts Incorporated. Member NASD/SIPC
3 Radnor Corporate Center, Suite 220 Radnor, PA 19087 (610) 995-1500

(THE PROGESSION OF WEALTH)

Table of Contents

Acknowledgements:

We would like to thank our clients, family, and friends who have entrusted us to accelerate their progress toward financial independence and our partners; Jack Blosky, CPA; Neil Dabagian, CPA; Brian Alten, CPA; and Scott Pontz and all our associates for their tireless dedication to our clients and the Progression of Wealth Process.

Special thanks to Heather Tracey for coordinating the project and to Brian O'Connell and his team for making the book come together.

October 2003

A Blueprint
for Achieving Wealth

"You can't always get what you want,
but if you try sometimes
you just might find
you get what you need."

– M. Jagger / K. Richards

December 1, 2003

OBIN SEWELL TUGGED DOWN HARDER on her baseball cap. She focused on breathing—two short breaths in, one long one out.

The 53 year-old entrepreneur, owner of her own public relations firm, held steady as she passed the five-mile marker. She hadn't noticed the mile marker—just the race volunteer, an elderly man in a nylon yellow wind-breaker with a bullhorn yelling "One mile to go! One mile!"

"Can't miss that," she thought to herself, gearing up for the last leg of the Philly Race for the Cure, a ten-kilometer race held every year since Robin had been in grade school in Center City Philadelphia. She'd run the race the year before for the first time and knew the race route well, having trained on it often during the past six months. Robin had read somewhere that there were four million miles of roads and streets in the US. In the last year, she'd joked to her husband, she felt like she'd run on every one of them. Then again, all that running would sure help her on the last mile—most of it up-hill—and leave something in her fuel tank. "I'll need some strength to open a beer later on," she thought. Still, she knew she would finish strong, especially upon spying her husband and two kids, Morgan and Jack, up ahead screaming and pointing to her.

She waved back, half-heartedly, to conserve some strength. Pulling closer she saw the sign her 21-year-old daughter Morgan had made. "Marathon Mom!" it said, in big, bold red stenciling. Jack, the 23-year-old, had grabbed it from Morgan, to her consternation, and was waving it wildly as she approached them, slowly but gamely. She picked up speed as she passed them, invigorated by their show of support. "Jumping Jack Flash!" her husband Roy yelled at her with arms pumping in the air. She laughed as she chugged on by; the Stones was Roy's favorite band. "Figures it'd be a Stones tune" she said under her breath.

Surging forward, buoyed by the crowd, she grabbed another cup of water from a little blond girl wearing an oversized Villanova sweatshirt. The girl was manning a table with paper cups full of water, and even more empty ones were scattered to the four winds by the runners who'd preceded Robin. She drank the cup greedily. Someone had told her once that the number one source of fatigue to the human body was lack of water. "Not today," she thought, flinging the cup to the ground harder than she had to. She'd made a habit of that, after all those years of watching the Boston Marathon and the Olympic runners doing the same thing. It gave her a rush, no denying that.

Picking her head up to gather more air into her lungs—a tip she'd gotten from a friend who ran marathons—she went into her finishing kick, the blue and white bunting framing the finish line now clearly in sight. The crowd had intensified closer to the finish line, all of them urging the runners on. Before she knew it, she saw the finish line and the digital clock ticking away on top of it. Running underneath it she heard the race director on her megaphone, calling off the times. "63.46 ... 63.48 ... 63.49." Robin ran under the banner at 63 minutes and 51 seconds, her best time yet. She allowed herself a clenched fist as she slowed down to a walk, gratefully accepting a bottle of water from another volunteer. "Congratulations!" he'd said. "Great job!" Too exhausted to do anything but mouth the words "thank you" she took her bottle and walked unsteadily toward the race tent, collapsing onto a picnic table seat, spent but happy. She'd done it again.

Minutes later Roy and the kids ambled in, Morgan and Jack making a beeline for the hot pretzel table. "Congratulations, honey," Roy said, giving her a warm hug. "I almost missed you back there at the bottom of the hill, you were such a blur. Nice going."

Robin looked up at him and smiled. "Jumping Jack Flash? What was that about?"

Roy grinned and shrugged his shoulders. "What can I say—a Rolling Stones classic that fit the occasion." He grabbed a bottle of water for himself and sipped some of it, enjoying the moment—the families and friends greeting the runners, the war stories already making the rounds from the tired but happy runners. "Wow! You've really come a long way," he said, shaking his head. "A long way."

Yes she had, Robin thought. They all had.

Her business was going great guns. After some fits and starts, the kids were doing great. With Roy's job as a senior vice president at a regional biotechnology firm located in Blue Bell, PA, which had two new drugs hit the market in the last year, the income was there, too. And, best of all, she had long ago stopped worrying about money and security, issues that had dogged her and her family for too many years. With Roy's job and Robin's burgeoning business, they didn't have to worry about money anymore like they used to . They didn't have to worry about running their bank accounts to zero, timing credit card payments, and checks clearing. Now they had cash reserves that they haven't dipped into in 10 years. The trouble was never money coming in. No, like most Baby Boomer couples, the problem was too much money going out. Now they had a big house in Blue Bell with a huge lot. A country club membership. Home theaters, two plush cars loaded with amenities, annual trips to Disney and the Caribbean, plenty of nights out for dinner and take-out when they decided to stay home. Heck, anything the Sewells wanted, they could now have. It wasn't always that way. Robin remembered when their Visa bill shot up to $4,000, then $5,000, then $6,000 per month. For a working couple making good money back then, they sure didn't have a lot left over every month for savings. Luckily, they hadn't had those kinds of worries for years.

Robin hadn't been too worried ten years ago either, though. With the stock market crash just a memory, and a bull market catching some steam, and Roy's fat stock options, their wealth kept on increasing—a trend she wrongly assumed would continue. Thankfully, Jay and Brian had pointed out early and often that the only true way to achieve financial independence is through time and diversification. It was a phrase she and Roy would hear often over the next decade. Another phrase they came to know, love and, at some times, hate, was that savings create wealth. So when what Alan Greenspan called "the era of irrational exuberance" began to wane, and the stock options and bonus money dried up for Roy, and the long line of entrepreneurs just dying to cut a check and hire Robin to handle their public relations began to thin out, the Sewells, with Jay and Brian's help, didn't miss a beat on their path toward financial independence.

At age 53 now, Robin reflected on the past ten years, on the financial troubles the couple had had, the overspending, the mammoth credit card bills, the fights about money . "Yep, we have come a long way," she thought. "And I can even remember the day we started to turn it all around. The day I first heard about The Progression of Wealth Process."

December 1, 1993 (ten years earlier) — The First Step in The Progression of Wealth

"Remember when Woody Allen said, 'Money is better than poverty, if only for financial reasons.'?"

Robin looked at Jay, somewhat suspiciously. Roy sat next to her, staring absent-mindedly at a painting on the office wall. Adjusting the strap of the pocket book she held in her lap, she shrugged her shoulders.

Jay, the financial advisor Roy and Robin's friend Erin had referred them to, seemed unfazed by their silence. He waited patiently while Roy and Robin grew more comfortable. He knew that most people coming to see him for the first time had a lot on their minds and weren't much more relaxed than they were when they visited the dentist. Jay winked at Brian Kohute, his partner at HJ Financial Group, the burgeoning financial practice Jay had founded in 1980 in a suburb of Philadelphia.

Brian cleared his throat and broke the silence "Yep, the Wood-man. Probably said that back when he was making funny movies." He turned toward Robin. "But the point is well taken. Money is everything in our culture. That's the first thing you've got to realize. In fact, Mrs. Sewell, money is so interwoven into our national culture that it has become the foundation on which we live our lives. Buying a house? You'll need money. Going to college? Money again. Care for luxuries like food and clothing? Three guesses on how you can obtain them."

She nodded. "That's why I'm here," she replied, pleasantly.

"Me, too," Roy added.

Jay nodded amiably. He knew. Things always started tentatively with new clients. That's why he and Brian always gave them what had come to be known inside the firm as the "Money Talk." It was an attention grabber—and getting a new client's attention was priority one with Jay. People always understood—and responded to—the power of money. He thought about news that had been making headlines that year. That was the first time the World Trade Center had been bombed by terrorists. There was a civil war raging in Somalia and the U.N. had sent in troops. And earlier that year, a standoff between a cult and authorities in Waco, Texas, had held the headlines.

But despite everything that was going on in the world, what was it that people liked to chat about at the water cooler or during their coffee breaks? The latest big lottery winners. How big the upcoming jackpot was. How many tickets they were planning to buy, and what they were planning to do with the winnings. It turned out that terrorist bombings, famine and civilian casualties, and crazed, gun-toting cult leaders were no match for the fateful numbers determining the winner of the next big pot.

Jay thought of that as he focused on Robin. She was his firm's archetypical client: between 40 and 60 years old; upper middle class. "We're so fixated on money that if Congress decided tomorrow to replace our national motto 'In God We Trust' with 'Early to bed, early to rise, until you make enough money to do otherwise,' would you really be that surprised? Heck, I wouldn't."

She smiled ruefully at the joke. "I wouldn't either."

Jay smiled at her. Progress, he thought. "But something's wrong with the way we treat money. Yes, we can't get enough of it. Yes, we worry about whether we have enough money or not. And yes, we want to be financially independent. But we also fear it. Like the two-ton elephant in the room that nobody wants to acknowledge, we're either unwilling or unable to take seriously the management of our money."

Roy looked up. "The unwillingness hasn't really been our problem," he said. "We want to manage our money better but we can't figure out how. Neither of us has a deep background in money management."

"We call that living in the Fragmented Finances Trap™," said Jay.

"What does that mean?" asked Robin.

"Most successful executives and business owners have achieved significant wealth, but they may still lack confidence in their future," said Jay. He started ticking off reasons on his fingers. "They don't have clear goals or a plan to achieve them. Their investments aren't organized, or they have the wrong insurance policies—maybe too much, maybe not enough. Or maybe their investment allocation won't allow them to achieve their goals. They're too risky or too conservative, or they may be taking on too much risk for the reward they might receive. Or else they don't fully understand their company benefits and aren't taking full advantage of their plans, or they are relying too much on their company stock. They are paying too much in taxes, their Wills are not complete or current, they do not have all their beneficiaries named, they use many advisors but the advisors are not being coordinated and do not work together. For these reasons, they are unnecessarily worried about their future, and not enjoying life as much as they could. This is why they are living in The Fragmented Finances Trap. Unfortunately, it's often a self-fulfilling prophecy because it's impossible to fix without a plan."

"Isn't that why we're here?" asked Robin.

Brian spoke up. "Sure. That's not to say you, or any other baby boomer in your situation, isn't concerned about money. You are. It's just that the concern hasn't triggered any action on the part of boomers to rectify the situation." Brian knew he was on firm ground. He'd seen study after study that said despite rising concerns over their ability to save money, especially in the face of rising health care costs and a sluggish economy, baby boomers hadn't taken much action to roll their sleeves up and go to work saving money. Just that week, he'd seen a study by Allstate Corporation on money and American baby boomers that said most baby boomers surveyed acknowledged worries about having sufficient retirement funds. And of the surveyed baby boomers who have not yet saved for retirement, the vast majority said that they could not afford to save for retirement, with most planning to start saving at a later date. How did the study conclude? With the ominous observation that boomers often operate without financial plans. They were all living in The Fragmented Finances Trap.

Brian paused to make sure Roy and Robin were on the same page. "Think about it, folks. How many of us can pinpoint the exact month and year that we will become financially independent? How many know exactly how their money is being spent each month and how much is going towards fulfilling their dreams of long-term financial independence? Most importantly, how many of us actually achieve those goals—a beach house in Florida; an around-the-world-trip; your own authentic Irish pub to run or your own gardening store to manage?" He stopped again to take a sip of coffee. "Hey, these are the daydreams of our youth, daydreams in our thirties and forties that turn into nightmares in our fifties and sixties when we realize we spent too much time on the dream and not enough time on the diligence needed to make our financial visions a reality. But that's what happens when you don't take action money-wise."

Both Roy and Robin sat quietly, content to let Jay and Brian do most of the talking. Robin knew they were right, but she didn't really feel their words were applicable to her own situation. After all, hadn't she and Roy done okay? Didn't they have a nice house, with a nice lot, and a Chevy Blazer and a Lexus in their two-car garage? Heck, they'd even managed to squirrel away a few bucks for the kids' college funds. Admittedly, it wasn't much. But it was something, wasn't it?

Jay sensed her disconnect. "How about a more concrete example? Roy, you play golf, right?"

Roy nodded. "Well, me too," said Jay. "But I bet you're like my golf buddies. Let me tell you a story. One day, after playing golf with a few friends, I got into a conversation with a fellow businessman; a successful entrepreneur who had built his own manufacturing company up from the ground floor. I knew him by reputation and considered him very successful, so when the topic of making money and investing came up, I noticed how closely our buddies were listening, just like in the old E. F. Hutton commercials. As he started giving advice on buying and selling stocks and playing the market, I realized what was happening. First, his advice was wrong, dangerous even. Second, *our friends were hanging on his every word!*"

He got up from behind his desk and wound around to the front of it. He leaned against it, making sure he had Roy and Robin's full attention. He had.

"I don't know what made me feel worse. The fact that this guy was willing to gamble his hard-earned money in such a cavalier and irresponsible way, leaving his family and loved ones vulnerable, or the fact that my friends were willing to leap into the abyss with him. The thing is, there are a million guys just like him."

Jay wanted to convince his new clients that he wasn't just blowing smoke. He needed their buy-in on how he was setting the table for them. He'd been a CPA and a financial advisor since 1977, spending his professional career helping people articulate and achieve their financial goals. He was accustomed to being involved in financial matters, to having people come to him for advice and information. Perhaps too accustomed. He had assumed that everyone either knows the basics of investment management, or had a professional relationship with someone who knows the basics of investment management. Just like he assumed with his golf buddies. But in that moment, he realized that what was crystal clear to him wasn't crystal clear to everybody else. What he knew about wealth creation and what he had come to take for granted was not very widely known at all.

Roy fidgeted, while Robin sat placidly, listening to Jay's story. "So . . . what does that have to do with our family's financial situation?"

"Well, what I found most surprising was that these were my peers—people like you and Roy. Same economic background. Same tax bracket. Same savvy business people. I mean, none of the guys I played golf with were selling pencils on the corner of State and Main Streets for a living, you know? None of them wore hairnets on the job and said things like 'Do you want fries with that?' Hell, no. They were all successful businessmen, and several of them had spouses who were high earners too. But for some reason, there was a detachment there. Not one of my buddies was applying his business savvy, fiscal responsibility, or personal commitment to his own portfolio. If they were, they wouldn't have been swooning like junior high school boys at a Madonna concert over a guy handing out dubious investment advice during a chance encounter at the golf club."

Robin cleared her throat and smiled back at Jay. Roy sat silently.

"After I got back from playing golf I huddled with Brian. I told him the story and pretty soon our blood was boiling. We started thinking about the hundreds of clients we've helped over the years. What has made so many of our clients so successful? How had they moved from where they typically were in our initial meeting, to their final achievement of financial independence? How did they turn their financial dreams into a reality? What was the common denominator?"

Robin folded her hands in her lap. "I know this is leading somewhere," she said. "Hopefully in a way that will help us."

Brian and Jay exchanged glances.

"Out of that meeting Brian and I began working on a financial planning process that applies directly to you, Robin, and to Roy and the rest of your family. Probably to a lot of your friends, too."

Brian took over. "We call it "The Progression of Wealth Process"—a process that will accelerate your progress toward financial independence—so you can make more money, enjoy life and achieve your goals, both personal and financial. We know it will help you make more money, enjoy life and achieve all your goals. Plus, it will free you from The Fragmented Finances Trap."

Roy tapped his fingers on the arm of his chair. "Hey, you guys are the professionals—that's why we're here. But I want to be clear on something. The last thing we want or need is some wacky investment scheme or some crazy day trading program." He eyed both of them steadily. "This progression of wealth process sounds good but only as long as it's solid and it works. I gotta tell you. I'm very concerned that we're not going to get to do the things that I thought we'd do in retirement. You know travel, buy a second home, things like that."

Jay spoke first. "It's going to take some time, Roy. But if you follow The Progression of Wealth Process, you'll be sitting on a beach somewhere sipping fancy drinks while you and Robin decide what four-star restaurant you'll be going to for dinner."

"Sounds good," Roy replied. "But we're the order-in types."

"That's good," Brian answered. "That type of financial outlook will come in handy over the next few years."

The Progression of Wealth Process™

Jay, Brian, Roy and Robin took a quick break. Roy walked outside to stretch his legs while Robin made a few calls. Jay and Brian huddled to discuss the Sewells' financial situation. After a few minutes Roy walked back into the office. Robin finished her calls and sat back down. Brian had gotten everyone a bottle of water. The Sewells were beginning to feel more comfortable.

"You know guys," Jay began. "Along with our national obsession over money is our alarming, for lack of a better word, relationship with financial debt. Ever hear of the comedian who said he'd received a note from his bank saying it hadn't received final payment on his loan? The cash-poor comedian wrote back 'Oh yes you have.'"

Robin laughed at the joke. "Don't I know it," she said. "I mean, it's not like we haven't struggled with finances and debt. Or, for that matter, studied up on it. I remember one Christmas where Roy and I wound up giving each other one of Jane Bryant Quinn's personal finance books. And I keep up with my mutual fund company's mailings, so I could keep track of what's going on in the financial world." She took a sip of water. "Don't know how much good it's done, though."

Jay nodded. "Hey, when it comes to money and debt, there are enough books to wallpaper the Great Wall of China." He knew that with consumer indebtedness at an all-time high and personal savings at an all-time low, it wasn't surprising that advice on getting out of debt, getting control of your finances, and getting over your subconscious aversion to money currently topped the book charts. Sure, these are good topics, he'd thought, especially for the authors who rake in the dough telling you stuff you already know— or ought to already know. But he wasn't interested in rehashing old themes with clients like the Sewells. Instead, he wanted to reveal to them the things most people didn't know about personal financial management—the things that financially independent families already know—like how to build a path to financial security. "We're really not interested in glitzy investment strategies," he added. "All we want to do is help you implement The Progression of Wealth Process *."

Roy nodded. "So, no speeches on the wealth creating powers of day trading, no-money-down commercial real estate investing, or some other get-rich-quick scheme?"

"Hell no," Brian said. "Look, get rich quick schemes and no-money-down real estate deals may make for a riveting read, but they have as much to do with serious wealth creation as do the tooth fairy and the ability of leprechauns to locate gold. What does create wealth is the development of a personalized plan for creating, growing, and then protecting wealth. Unfortunately, so few Americans actually have such a plan. And of those who do, even fewer stick with it." Brian told Roy and Robin about another study he had seen recently, this one by the GE Center for Financial Learning, where only seven percent of baby boomers had an adequate long term care insurance plan in place. He'd mentioned another boomer study from MarketResearch.com which said that fewer than 44 percent of boomers have financial investments of any kind, and only 27 percent have a 401(k) plan for retirement. "Due to such poor saving habits," he said, "over 75 percent of all boomers will continue working beyond the traditional retirement age of 65. We don't want that to happen to you, unless, that is, you want to work in retirement."

Robin glanced at Roy and plunged ahead. "What we want, Brian, is to be able to make our own choices," she answered.

"Fine. That's what we want, too," said Jay. "And The Progression of Wealth Process is your ticket there."

Roy sighed. "Okay, okay, what is this progression of wealth process you keep talking about?"

"Ahh, our favorite subject. With The Progression of Wealth Process, it's the process and the plan that count," said Brian. "But what do we mean by it? 'Progression' is defined as 'the act of moving towards a goal.' In your case, it is the road from the beginning of one's financial life—launching a career, starting a family, creating a portfolio—to the end—a secure and active retirement, well-educated children adequately prepared for the world, and a peaceful enjoyment of the fruits of your labors over the years. It is the road that so many of your fellow baby boomers are traveling right now, but in many cases without a map."

Jay cleared his throat and popped a lozenge into his mouth. "Cold season. Damn." He sat back down in his seat, directly opposite Roy and Robin.

"Musically, when folks use the term *progression*, it refers to a series of repetitions that take place with a definite pattern of advance," Jay said. "This is critical. Even as you create a plan, life changes. You plan for two children, and ten years later, you're blessed with a surprise pregnancy. You pay off your house, and your job offers you a raise and a promotion, but you have to relocate to a more expensive part of the country. Your elderly parent needs specialized medical care and requires financial assistance from you to obtain it. Your spouse has a mid-life crisis, quits his high-powered corporate job, and goes back to art school to become a painter—at a third of his previous salary. Still, he's happier than you've ever seen him and that's what really counts."

Jay fiddled with a rubber band that he was stretching between his fingers. "But you know, life happens this way. Determining your path to financial independence requires both a plan and a process for maintaining and updating that plan. Why a plan? Well, like John Belushi said in the movie *Animal House* 'Why not?'"

Robin smiled at the reference. She loved the movie. She recalled arranging for a baby-sitter so that she and Roy could see it. She looked over at Roy who was already chuckling over the comment.

"But without a plan you're doomed," Jay continued. "Let me ask you something. Suppose you were on a non-stop flight from San Francisco to Tokyo. You've just taken off and the captain introduced his flight plan over the intercom. 'Ladies and gentlemen, this is your captain speaking. We're traveling west across the Pacific Ocean. In a few hours you'll look down and see land. When that occurs, we'll start looking for a big city with an airport. If we find one before our fuel runs out, we'll land. Then we'll figure out where we are and decide what we want to do next. In the meantime, just sit back, relax, and enjoy your flight.' I don't know about you, but I wouldn't be relaxed. Hell, I'd be looking for the liquor cart."

Roy laughed. Robin leaned back in her chair. Both were finally beginning to relax. Maybe they were in good hands after all, thought Robin. Maybe.

"But that's why you need a plan—and that's what The Progression of Wealth Process offers," he added. "It's a built-in way to regularly review and revise your plan to accommodate change, where we can help you effectively manage life's curve balls, and still make progress towards your long-term goals. When we don't, we are relying on luck—just like that clueless pilot I just told you about."

The Progression of Wealth Process: An Overview

Stage One – The Progression of Wealth Blueprint: The purpose of the blueprint is to help you determine what your goals are, the amount of money that will be needed to accomplish those goals, the opportunities that you may look forward to in life, the strengths that you have to help you achieve these goals, and the risk that you feel are involved in making this process happen.

Stage Two – The Report Card: Once you've discovered your goals, the purpose of The Report Card is to determine where you currently stand in The Progression of Wealth Process. Remember grade school? Each year or half-year you received a report card from the school telling you and your parents how you fared as a student. Later on in your professional career, you probably saw much the same idea with your employee evaluation. But when in your financial life did you ever receive a report card? You will now.

The Financial Independence Cultivator: The purpose of the Financial Cultivator is to develop a specific action plan that will allow you to meet all your short-term goals, which are the goals you want to achieve within the next five years.

Stage Three – The Investment Portfolio Optimizer: evaluates your investment portfolio to determine whether your asset allocation is appropriate for the return needed to meet your goals. In addition, the risk inherent in your portfolio is evaluated and compared to your Risk Profile to ensure you are comfortable with the amount of risk being taken. The goal of The Investment Portfolio Optimizer is to optimize the return needed for you to meet your goals while taking the least amount of risk. You will have an asset allocation specifically tailored to you and your goals.

The Cash Flow Optimizer: unlocks your savings power. The Cash Flow Optimizer is a both a diagnostic and budgeting tool. It will determine your opportunities to save more, or spend (gift) more, if appropriate. In addition, the Cash Flow Optimizer projects future cash flows to determine the effects on your Progression of Wealth.

Stage Four – The Financial Independence Expander: takes the power of The Investment Portfolio Optimizer and The Cash Flow Optimizer and culminates in the development of the recommendations and action steps to meet your medium and long-term goals: a concise executive summary and a detailed analysis explaining the Milestone (goal), the amount required to fund the goal, and the specific recommendations and action plan required to achieve the Milestone.

Stage Five - The Wealth Protector: is a comprehensive evaluation of all the risks that threaten you and your wealth. The Wealth Protector ensures that you, your family, and your assets are protected. Your risk management philosophy will be developed and your current insurance evaluated to determine if you have the right coverage(s) and plans in place, or if there are gaps in coverage.

The Estate Planner: helps structure your wealth to ensure that your loved ones are provided for and that your wealth passes to your loved ones and favorite charities efficiently and effectively while paying the least amount of taxes legally possible.

The Loved Ones' Letter: is a document that instructs your family and friends on exactly who to contact in case of an emergency and includes a comprehensive list of all your assets, liabilities, insurance policies, trust documents, and Wills. The Loved Ones' Letter provides peace of mind for the family member who is not primarily responsible for the personal finances.

Stage Six – The Income Tax Strategy : ensures that taxes are being reduced to the lowest amount legally possible. Throughout the year your tax situation is being monitored and evaluated to ensure that you are taking advantage of every tax-deferred savings vehicle and tax deduction possible. It also provides you peace of mind that your tax return was prepared and reviewed by experienced CPAs who will represent you if selected for an IRS Audit.

Brian took out a blue binder. Embossed on the cover were the words "The Progression of Wealth." He handed it to Robin. "Yeah, we know. Where's the beef, right? That binder is your Progression of Wealth." He took out his own copy and opened it up. "Here's where we want to start. Next time we will complete The Progression of Wealth Blueprint. And don't forget to start lining up the documents we'll need to get started. The list of what we need is on the document request list." (Located on page 15.)

She accepted the binder and placed it on her lap. "Is this going to mean a drastic change for us?" she asked. "You know, restricted budgets, macaroni and cheese for dinner every night, buying my clothes at the church bazaar. I really hate velour."

Roy nodded and made a face. "No velour."

Jay chuckled. "No, nothing that severe. But there will be some change. It's all good, though." He snapped the rubber band he was fooling around with and shot it across the room. "Besides, change is good. And you can't wait to change. Did you know that a frog can sit in a pot of water and not notice the temperature rise to the boiling point? Some people are like that in their financial lives. They ignore changes occurring in their environment, and by the time they wake up, they're boiled."

Brian sat back, waiting patiently for Jay to finish.

"The 'change' thing is up to you," Brian said. "No book or financial advisor can get you to delve into your personal finances if you're not ready and willing to do it. A management consultant I once knew specialized in working with Fortune 100 corporations that were trying to make significant changes to the vision and mission of their organization. Usually, the very existence of their business was dependent on the changes taking place. Still, he found the

The Progression of Wealth™
HJ Financial Group
Certified Public Accountants
Business and Personal Financial Advisors

Document Checklist

Please bring the documents listed below to The Progression of Wealth Process Blueprint™ meeting.
If you bring originals, we will copy them and return the originals to you.

☐ Prior year's Tax Return (Last two years)

☐ W2 Statement(s) and/or copies of the most recent payroll statements

☐ Net Worth Statement, if available (worksheet attached)

☐ Annual/Monthly Budget or estimate of living expenses (worksheet attached)

☐ Copies of most recent Bank, Brokerage, and/or Mutual Fund Statements

☐ Copies of all Insurance Policies
    (life, health, disability, long-term care, homeowner, and auto)

☐ Copies of Retirement Plan Statements
    (IRAs, Pension Plans, 401k Plans, SEPs, Simple, Keogh, etc.)

☐ Copies of current Wills and Trust documents

☐ Copies of any Gift Tax Returns filed

☐ Investor Profile Questionnaire (booklet attached)

☐ Copy of Employee Benefits Manual

☐ List of Investments available within company's retirement plan

1000 Germantown Pike, Suite H-1, Plymouth Meeting, PA 19462
610 . 272 . 4700   Fax: 610 . 272 . 6785
www.hjfinancialgroup.com

people managing and running the organizations always seemed to resist and sabotage the changes, even though they knew they were the only thing that might save them. That reluctance to change can prove costly. In 1950, Britain made 80 percent of the world's motorcycles. Today it makes less than one percent. Triumph, the country's leading motorcycle manufacturer, clung to old, inefficient production methods. The trouble was, its competitors didn't. American and Japanese motorcycle makers like Harley Davidson and Honda modernized their facilities, changing to more techno-savvy production methods, and wound up making better and cheaper motorcycles. In the process, they left Triumph choking in the dust."

Roy and Robin got up and picked their coats up. "So, I guess the moral of the story is change and prosper?" Robin asked.

Jay looked over at Brian. "She learns quick. Resist change and wither on the vine."

"Okay, no vine-withering for us," she said, walking to the door with Roy. "We'll see you in a week and we'll start progressing our way to wealth."

When you have completed The Progression of Wealth Process you will:

- Have clear goals and a plan to achieve them
- Have investments that are organized and properly allocated
- Have an investment program in place that enables you to achieve your goals
- Have found the fast-track to financial independence
- Be making more money, enhancing your lifestyle, and achieving your personal and financial goals

Introduction Overview:
The Progression of Wealth Process™ Defined

The Progression of Wealth Process helps accelerate your progress toward financial independence. It will help you make more money, enhance your lifestyle and achieve your goals—both personal and financial.

Once you have completed The Progression of Wealth Process, you will have accelerated your progress toward financial independence. You will have a clear vision of your future and a plan to achieve it. In addition, you will be able to save more money, your assets will be properly allocated, structured, and protected, your investment portfolio will be optimized to maximize your return and minimize your risk, you will have a comprehensive risk management and estate plan, you will have reduced your taxes, and you will never have to worry about money again. But most important, you will be making more money, enhancing your lifestyle, and achieving your goals— personal and financial.

PLANNING YOUR PERSONAL PROGRESSION TO WEALTH

"Your time has come to shine,
All your dreams are on their way."

— Paul Simon

June 21, 2003

ROY SEWELL EXPERTLY TWISTED THE CORKSCREW into the bottle of Merlot, pressing down firmly, but not too hard, turning the device clockwise until the screw was no longer visible. Then he took the metal wings of the corkscrew and pressed down firmly on both of them until the cork popped out easily.

Whistling softly to himself he poured the Merlot into two big wine glasses, being careful not to pour too much or too little. He remembered his bartending days back in college, when his boss, Mrs. Green, would come around every so often and eyeball the amount of wine he would pour into a glass or measure the level of a martini he'd made. "There's an art to pouring a cocktail," she'd said. "People notice if you don't pour it right."

He carried both glasses out onto the deck, where Robin was sunbathing. The villa on Hutchinson Island, about an hour north of Palm Beach, Florida, was a steal at $1,500 for the week. Such a steal, in fact, that Roy and Robin decided to stay for two weeks.

"Here you go, Hon," Roy said, placing the glass on the glass table next to her deck chair.

"Thanks, Roy," she answered. "The kids still down at the pool?"

"Yep. Having a great time. Jack is surrounded by girls in bikinis and Morgan has already struck up a conversation with a lifeguard on the beach." Roy had decided to watch her closely. You could never be too careful with a 20-year-old daughter.

Robin sighed contentedly. The biggest decision they'd have to make tonight was whether to drive over the causeway to Jenson Beach for dinner or just go downstairs and eat at Shuckers, the resort's restaurant and bar. "How'd you hit 'em today, Roy?"

"Not bad," said Roy. "Shot an 82 on the south course. Had two birdies on the back nine, too." He swung an imaginary 9-iron, a la Johnny Carson.

Robin smiled. "I'm so glad we found this place. It's heaven."

Roy nodded. "Yeah, and we got a good deal on it, too. We'll have to come back here next year. Maybe go up to Disney. Orlando's only two hours north of here, you know."

"You've been saying that for the past seven years but we've never repeated a vacation yet," Robin teased him.

"We haven't missed a vacation or two or three in the past seven years either," answered Roy.

"Hey, I'm definitely not complaining," said Robin "We just seem to pick nicer and nicer vacation spots every time."

"Yep," agreed Roy, "we have been lucky—not one bad vacation in the past seven years—or is it eight years? But who's counting anyway?"

Robin laughed and let her mind wander. She thought back to the times when vacations like this were few and far between. But not anymore, she thought to herself. Not after the Progression of Wealth. She thought back to when she and Roy had just met Jay and Brian and had started The Progression of Wealth Process.

December 15, 1993 (ten years earlier) — What Do You Want to Achieve with Your Wealth?

Roy and Robin walked into HJ Financial Group's office. It was a brisk, cold day and, with the holidays near, no one was in business mode except Jay and Brian. They were warmly greeted by HJ's associate, Heather, and shown to the conference room, where they accepted the offer of coffee.

Jay and Brian came in and shook hands with the Sewells. Roy pointed to the tape recorder in the middle of the table and asked, "What are we doing here today?"

Brian explained. "We prefer to tape the first session so we can focus our attention on listening rather than taking notes. We then can go back and listen to the tape to ensure we don't miss anything. Is that okay with you?" Roy and Robin both nodded.

Jay opened a large colorful document and said, "Who wants to go first?"

Roy volunteered to go first and Jay asked "What do you want to achieve with your wealth ... in the next year? In other words, if we were sitting here one year from today what would have to have happened with your wealth for you to think the year was a success?"

Roy paused for what seemed like an eternity. There was complete silence. Roy stammered, not sure what to say, and Jay simply repeated the question; "If we were sitting here one year from today what would have to have happened with your wealth for you to think the year was a success?"

Roy thought again, then said, "Well, we need to start saving more. I would like to cover the kids' education, especially high school and college."

"Great," Jay said. "Robin, what about you?"

Robin took a deep breath. "We need to have the kitchen remodeled. There, I said it. It was hard for me to say because this has always been a point of contention between Roy and me. Roy never wants to put money into the house. He would let it run into the ground."

Roy tried to chime in, but Jay stopped him and said smilingly, "You'll get your turn to speak again. Anything else, Robin, that you want to achieve with your wealth?

"Yes. I agree with Roy we need to cover private high school for the children. I want to feel secure over the next year. I think it would be great to accomplish this over the next year—if that's ... well ... possible."

Jay then said, "Okay, Robin, what do you want to achieve with your wealth over the next 5 years? If we were sitting here 5 years from now, and your kitchen had been remodeled, you had provided for private high school education for your children and you felt secure, what else has to happen with your wealth over the next 5 years for you to think it was a success?"

"Hmmm! These are good questions!" said Robin, pausing to sip some coffee. "I guess that over 5 years, if Roy let me do the kitchen, I want to start my own business. I would like to put a pool in the yard. I would also like to begin family vacations for 2 weeks a year."

"Great," Jay said. "These are good, concrete goals. How about you, Roy?"

"Let's see," said Roy. "I want to have Jack's college education covered. I would like to rent a house on the beach for a month a year and I want to make sure retirement is on track."

"Excellent!" proclaimed Jay "You're both getting the hang of it now. Now Roy, what if we go out ten years? You were able to achieve all your 5 year goals, what else has to happen with your wealth over the next ten years?"

Roy started musing aloud. "Let's see. I will be 55 in 10 years. By then, I want to be done paying for college education for both kids. I maybe want to own a property at the shore rather than renting. Of course, I would need a boat to go with the house. I also would think of downsizing our current house since the kids will be outta there. Of course, I will be thinking about retirement pretty heavily, so I want to know it will be doable when I am 60."

"Good, anything beyond the ten years?"

"Well sure, I want to retire when I am 60. I would like to help the kids, like maybe a down payment for their first homes. It would also be great to help with the grandchildren's education if we could. I've always wanted to leave my mark on the world, like a family legacy." Roy set down his coffee cup and took a deep breath. Roy had lost both his parents at an early age and he wanted to make sure he provided for his kids and their kids, so the subject was very important to him.

Robin broke the somberness a moment later when she said, "A boat, Roy! You don't know anything about boating. Didn't you get seasick when you went fishing with your brother and the kids?"

Jay took that mood change as an opportunity to finish the money talk with Robin. "What do you want to accomplish over the next 10 years and beyond?"

"Well, I also think we need to be ready to pay for our daughter's wedding."

Roy chimed in. "In the next 10 years—oh my God! Not if I have anything to say about it! Although she's always giggling with her friends about boys, so I wouldn't be surprised if it happened in the next ten years."

Jay asked if there was anything else. "I would like to continue traveling but now maybe 4 weeks a year rather than 2 weeks. Also, we may need to provide for my parents. They could need our help if one of them needs care later in life," said Robin.

Jay asked her, "Anything beyond the 10 years?"

"Sure, I would like be able to help our kids and hopefully grandchildren and then charities. I want to be there for our kids. Most of all I want to have a secure and happy life. We have a good life now, and I want that to continue. Maybe even to get better."

"That was great work, guys," Jay congratulated them. "Now our job is to begin The Progression of Wealth Process that will allow you to educate your children, buy the second home and boat, retire, create a family legacy and most of all live a great, happy, and secure life. And The Progression of Wealth Process will get us there. But before we get started we need to get very specific about all the goals we discussed so far.

"The first goal was to redo the kitchen," said Jay. "What will it cost to have the kitchen redone?"

Roy said, "No more than $5,000[1]."

"Oh, please Roy!" snapped Robin. "It will cost $10,000[1] to $15,000[1] easily."

"What!" It was Roy's turn to be aggravated. "No way are we spending that for the kitchen."

Jay and Brian were veteran financial advisors and had seen similar debates before. They quickly refereed a compromise. "Let's put $15,000 down and see how this fits with your other goals," Brian suggested. Roy and Robin agreed, he grudgingly, she a tad smugly. "When do you want to have the kitchen done by?" asked Jay"

"By the fall would be nice. Like the end of October of next year," said Robin.

"The next goal is high school education for your children. Tell us what kind of education you would like to provide for your children?" asked Brian.

"That's easy," said Robin. "I went to private school and we would like to send our children to private school as well."

"What is that going to cost in today's dollars?" asked Jay.

"Oh boy ... I guess $5,000[2] per year," answered Robin with a furrowed brow.

"Try $7,000[2]," quipped Roy.

---

1 After considering the effects of inflation, these amounts would be $15,000, $30,000, and $45,000, respectively, in 2003 dollars.

2 In today's dollars (2003) the average cost of private high school is $15,000 per year and the average cost of private college is $30,000 per year.

"You're probably closer on-track with that figure," Brian said. "When will the kids be in school?"

"Jack will start high school next year in September of '94, and Morgan two years later in September of '96."

"How about college?"

"We want to give our kids the ability to go to whatever college they choose, so I'm sure that's gonna mean big bucks," said Roy. "How much would you guys estimate that would cost?"

"I would think that, by the time they're in school, we should estimate it at approximately \$20,000[3] per year," said Brian.

"Yow. Can you see me starting to sweat?" quipped Roy.

"Jack is starting in 1998 and Morgan in 2000," said Robin. "So at least that is a few years away."

"What about your business, Robin?" asked Jay.

"Well, I had a career in public relations before we started a family and I really enjoyed it, Robin began.

Roy jumped in and said, "And she was great at it."

Robin smiled at him. "I think it might cost about \$50,000 to get it up and running but I'm really not sure," she continued.

"When would you like to start the business?" asked Brian.

"I think in about two years," said Robin firmly. "Wow. I've never really admitted to myself out loud when I wanted to start doing this. I've never put a price tag or start date on it. Before it was just a dream."

Jay smiled. "Then we're definitely moving in the right direction."

"It's scary, but invigorating," said Robin. "I wonder if I can actually run a successful business. I just realized that you're asking us to put dates on things to make them seem more tangible and real. It feels good."

"Robin and I have never delved deep into our wishes. But it's nice to know our goals overlap," said Roy.

"I want to reiterate that The Progression of Wealth Process will ensure that we establish a game plan for each milestone and implement the steps to ensure you achieve them," said Jay. After Jay finished capturing their milestones and amounts needed he flipped over the Blueprint.

---

3 In today's dollars (2003) the average cost of private high school is \$15,000 per year and the average cost of private college is \$30,000 per year.

Risks — Opportunities — Strengths

"We need to have the wake-up-at-2:00-in-the-morning talk," said Jay.

"Okay," said Robin cautiously. "What does that mean?"

"You know—those things that wake you up in the middle of the night that scare you. Those major risks you are facing that you must try to manage to an acceptable level," Jay explained.

"I don't think anything wakes Roy up in the middle of the night," said Robin, "even when the kids were little and screaming."

"I sleep pretty soundly, but since you've brought it up, I'll probably start waking up at 2 a.m. from now on," said Roy.

"My biggest fear is my parents' health," said Robin. "I'm worried about what would happen if one of them has to go into a nursing home."

"Plus, with an 11-year-old and a 13-year-old in the house and the economy and stock market so unpredictable, unemployment is always a scary thought," added Roy.

"I guess my real biggest concern is not being there for the kids," said Robin thoughtfully.

"Okay," Jay said, "staying on the wake-up-at-2:00-in-the-morning theme, what wakes you up in the middle of the night with your heart pounding causing you to say, "we have such great opportunities ahead of us, we have to take advantage of them?" Any opportunities like that you see ahead of you?" asked Jay.

"Sure. My wife going into business for herself is a great opportunity for us. Also, my stock options could be a huge benefit if the market continues to move ahead. We are both hard workers, so I think our ability to earn a living and enjoy ourselves is a great advantage we have," said Roy.

"Excellent!" said Jay. "What brings it all together is the strengths you both have. What strengths will you rely on to help you meet all the goals you have?" he asked.

Without hesitation, Roy said, "Robin's ability to make money in public relations."

"And the fact that Roy is a great provider, which allowed me to work part-time and stay at home raising the kids," added Robin. "That was important to me. I didn't want a stranger raising our kids. So that has been a tremendous strength for us. Roy is a good leader and manager of people. I hope nothing ever happens to his company, but his skills make him very employable."

"That was great," said Jay. "The fact that you're so focused about these things is making it easier for all of us. Obviously, a big part of The Progression of Wealth Process will be to manage and minimize your risks to an acceptable level. Unfortunately, you cannot eliminate all risks and you certainly can't ignore them, but you can reduce them dramatically."

"Also, we will take advantage of the opportunities you have in front of you and we will build and draw on your strengths that have gotten you this far. Make sense?" asked Brian.

"Sure," said Roy and Robin, overlapping each other.

"We are almost finished with the Blueprint," said Brian. "The last step is to go through all the financial documents that we asked you to bring so we don't miss anything. Roy asked why they needed to bring them all to the first meeting. Well, quite frankly, it shows your level of commitment to your personal finances. Our experience has proven to us that clients who take the time to gather all their documents are serious about moving forward with their financial plan, whereas those who come empty-handed will always have a reason or excuse why they can't implement recommendations that will help them achieve financial independence."

"You're right!" said Roy. "We met with a financial planner about two years ago. He asked us some questions about our assets, liabilities, income, and expenses and sent us a canned financial plan that killed about 10 trees to produce. We still have it in our attic. We definitely were not committed at the time and we wasted his time and our own. Not to mention money."

"Well that's it for this time," said Jay. "At the next meeting, we'll cover the Report Card and The Financial Independence Cultivator."

"Sounds good to me," said Roy. "Looks like we're off to a good start."

After the meeting, Robin excused herself and headed out to pick up the kids.

"She's great," said Brian. "Seems really focused and like a real tough cookie."

"She sure is," Roy agreed. He leaned back in his chair. "So I wanted to ask you. Why did you guys focus so much on our goals and so little on our actual investments so far?"

Jay answered. "Setting goals is the key ingredient to creating wealth. The cultural landscape is loaded with success stories that were set in motion by goal setting. Take a look at Steven Jobs for instance, the founder of Apple Computer. When Jobs was 12 years old, he had the gumption to call Bill Hewlett, founder of Hewlett-Packard, and ask him for some expensive computer parts. Amused at the young lad's temerity, Hewlett sent him the parts."

Roy whistled. "Damn. I wouldn't have known what to do with computer parts at age twelve. Hell, I still don't know what to do with a whole computer, let alone the computer parts."

"Or how about advertising legend David Ogilvy?" Brian jumped in. "Ogilvy, once a small tobacco farmer in Pennsylvania, had scraped some cash together and started what he was sure to be the world's greatest advertising agency. The first thing Ogilvy did after hanging out his shingle was to make a list of the five clients he wanted most. The list, which included General Foods and Shell Oil, among others, was checked off one by one until Ogilvy had them all."

"Setting goals for you, by and large, works the same way as it did for Jobs and Ogilvy," explained Jay. "Like any good traveler, embarking on a journey will take you along a predetermined path. Your path should lead you to financial security. But before you create an investment strategy you've got to lay out some goals to reach and then create a timeline for reaching them. The goals should also be tailored to your personal financial situation.

Advantages of Goal-Setting

A 2002 study by American Express Retirement Services reports that, despite miserable economic conditions and roiling financial markets, Americans who establish long-term financial planning goals are a significantly better bet to create wealth and reach financial security. According to the study, people who set financial goals felt more confident and were better prepared to withstand tough economic times. Correspondingly, 45% of study participants who didn't set financial goals felt they wouldn't reach financial security unless they received professional advice from a financial advisor.

Source: Financial Planning Interactive: The Confidence Game, November 1, 2002

Like anything else in your life, your financial situation is fluid and dynamic, changing with life events like a new job, a new marriage, a new baby, a new house."

"But why all the fuss about specific goal-setting?" Roy asked. "We just want our money to grow. Isn't that really everyone's goal?"

"Well, some common denominators exist in financial goal setting," Jay replied. "Everyone has their own value system, and what's important to you may not be important to the guy down the hall in accounting or the woman who teaches history at your local high school. But if you can determine what your values are—to retire early, to travel the world, or to run your own small business—and then set about defining goals to help you meet those lifestyle values, it makes it much easier to create a financial plan that works for you. That's what our goal is for you, anyway."

Roy turned to Jay. "Well it makes sense. But how are you supposed to achieve your goals when things keep changing all the time? I mean, I've got two kids going to college in the next five to seven years, a wife who wants to start her own business, and a mother-in-law who's going to need to go into senior housing pretty damn soon. I've got to deal with all that and set goals, too?"

Jay nodded. "I hear you. All I can say is that when defining your goals and dreams, try to be realistic. If you're idea of wealth originates from what you

Lifetime Goals

The following is a list of typical areas in our lives that our goals grow out of and some of the directions they can point us to:

- *Physical: health, fitness, physical well-being*
- *Spiritual: faith, community, sense of wholeness, values, philanthropy*
- *Mental: learning, art, culture, conversation*
- *Travel: vacation, cultural experiences, visiting friends and family*
- *Recreation: leisure time, hobbies, balance of work and play*
- *Home: your base, your castle, your artist's canvas*
- *Career: next steps, changing technology, fresh start, new business*
- *Relationships: friends, family, community, how you want to be in the world*

read in *Town & Country* magazine or from that biography that you saw on David Bowie on VH-1, that's not realistic. More likely, it's fantasy. Instead, let your goals reflect who you really are."

"How many of us plan our lives this way—setting artificial goals that have nothing to do with our passions, our dreams, and our lifestyles? More than any of us would like to admit, I'm sure," Brian added.

"One last point about goal-setting. It's good to remember that happiness, wealth, and success are only the by-products of goal-setting—they're not the goals themselves," said Jay.

Jay wanted to leave Roy with a few last thoughts on planning and goal setting.

"You know, Roy, John Lennon once said that life is what happens when you're waiting for something else," Jay said. "He was right. Despite our best planning, life happens. Things change—the economy takes a turn up or down, we have extra babies, we take new jobs—all the stuff that makes life

Did You Know? ...

... *That the average American will have only 37% of the yearly income they'll require to live on in retirement?*

... *That, on average, Americans will live 30 years as retirees?*

... *That Americans are saving 50% less than they were in 1980?*

... *That, due to inflation, it only takes 20 years for the value of your money to be cut in half?*

... *That your Social Security benefits are in great peril? In the 1950s, 16 Americans were paying into Social Security for each American collecting Social Security. By 2030 that ratio will be 2/1.*

... *That health care costs are rising at twice the rate of the Consumer Price Index?*

... *That college costs are growing at twice the rate of inflation?*

All the more reason to create a plan for wealth creation—so you can withstand these challenges and live a comfortable life in retirement.

Source: Huntington Retirement Guide

Wealth Progression Timeline

A wealth progression timeline enables you to infuse your goals with reality, so that when you move into the planning phases you have a complete picture of what lies ahead:

Ages 31-40. *You may be into your second or third (and more expensive) home. Children are being born, getting older, getting more expensive. Protection of income becomes even more important now that there are more dependants. Possibly working against you is the loss of a second income as one parent remains at home with young children, and expenditures on maintaining the children. Consequently, you're probably feeling financially pinched by now, even if you're earning more. However, don't suspend making contributions to your retirement fund. If it comes down to a choice between funding college or funding retirement, retirement should take priority. Kids can always find other methods to finance their way through college. No one else is going to pay for your retirement. Update your Will, if necessary, and periodically review your life insurance to make sure it is adequate, especially if you have children.*

Ages 41-50. *Income-wise, these are your salad days. So keep socking away money for retirement. One thing to consider at this stage is aging parents. Will they be able to financially take care of themselves should they need home health care or a nursing home? Or will you be expected to pay some of the bill? Consider buying long-term care insurance for them if they can't afford it. Discuss with them their potential financial needs and concerns. Make sure their estate plan is in place.*

Ages 51-60. *Expenses may start to ease off in this stage as your children reach maturity and, you hope, move out of the house. Beef up your retirement contributions to at least 15 percent, maybe 20 percent or more, of your income. This will probably be the last good stretch to really sock it away. Start getting serious about your vision of retirement, too. It will make a difference in how you plan. Don't get too conservative in your investing at this stage, even if you plan to retire soon. You've got a lot of years of living left and plenty of time to weather market ups and downs. Get serious about an estate plan.*

Ages 61-70. *Study your Social Security and Medicare options to make sure you take full advantage of them. Be sure you don't have gaps in medical coverage if you retire before you're qualified for Medicare. Consider working part-time in retirement. A rocking chair can get boring after a while. Buy long-term care insurance if you haven't already. Carefully review retirement plan payout options. How you choose is immensely important. Absolutely have an estate plan. Investments should not be too conservative; with good health, you'll have many years left to live in retirement and you'll need your nest egg to stay ahead of inflation.*

Ages 70 and beyond. *Hey, slow down and enjoy. You've earned it! Talk to your kids about your estate and update your Will so it's in line with new circumstances. Grandchildren are likely already on the scene, so inheritance tax planning and related subjects may have to be considered from a different viewpoint.*

worth living. Your blueprint takes this into account by assessing opportunities, strengths, and risks that could have an impact on your goals."

Brian added, "For opportunities, we asked you what might help support your achievement of these goals. For example, do you feel fairly certain that in five more years you will receive a promotion with a substantial pay raise? Do you anticipate an inheritance within the next ten years that will change your financial situation? You have to look at current or anticipated events that might be opportunities for you. When you incorporate this into your goals, you become better at spotting and taking advantage of unforeseen opportunities down the road."

"Brian's right," Jay said. "All of us have traits, qualities, and circumstances that work in our favor, whether we realize it or not. Identifying your particular strengths enables you to make the most of them. Are you particularly focused and tenacious? Then you can plan to withstand challenges that perhaps others would not, and maybe you can be more aggressive in your plan. Do you have an advanced degree or a unique set of skills that make you particularly valuable in your field? Filter what you know about your unique skills, talents, and attributes through a financial lens and determine which will serve you best in the future."

"And, let's face it, we each take a risk every time we cross the street, drive our car too fast down a winding road, get in an airplane," said Brian. "Risks are a part of life, whether they are calculated or random. We can anticipate some of what life might throw our way and use a solid planning process to at least minimize the negative impact down the road. When you discussed the risks you feel you are facing in the years to come, you mentioned job loss and untimely death of a spouse. Managing these risks has to become part of your financial plan because they could have a significant impact on your goals."

Roy nodded his head. " Okay, now I'm starting to see why The Progression of Wealth starts with setting goals."

"It has to," said Jay, smiling, "because it ends with you achieving those goals."

"Point taken," said Roy with a grin.

Rating Your Financial Compatibility

Studies show that money is the single biggest cause of arguments and disagreements among couples. That's too bad, as couples, seeking harmony, often avoid discussing money and finances, leading to more problems and unfortunate surprises down the road. To help bridge the communications gap, the New York State Society of CPAs has created the following financial compatibility quiz:

Answer "true" or "false" to each of the following statements:

1 *We are aware of and comfortable with each other's money personalities.*

2 *We have discussed our short- and long-term financial goals.*

3 *My spouse and I are well-versed in personal finance.*

4 *My spouse and I have discussed a plan to structure our finances.*

5 *We have planned for the impact that marriage will have on our taxes.*

6 *We have decided how to divide up the money management tasks.*

7 *We understand the importance of establishing a realistic budget.*

8 *I know my future spouse's investment personality and risk tolerance.*

9 *I know how much debt my spouse is bringing into our marriage.*

10 *We have made a commitment to discuss money regularly.*

According to the NYSCPA, if you ...

... answered "true" to eight or more statements indicates that you and your spouse are on your way to a stable financial future. However, it's still a good idea to continue to communicate and work together.

... answered "true" to between five and seven of the above statements, you and your spouse need to devote more time to planning your financial future together. With a little luck, you can achieve financial compatibility.

... answered "true" to fewer than five questions, don't call off the wedding yet. Instead, make a sincere commitment to discuss these issues and consider meeting with an experienced financial planner who can help you start your marriage on firm financial footing.

Source: New York Society of CPAs

Chapter 1 Overview:
Setting the Stage for The Progression of Wealth™

Goal-setting is a critical component for The Progression of Wealth Process. Setting goals for your own plan, by and large, works the same way. Like any good traveler, embarking on a journey will take you along a predetermined path. Your path should lead you to financial security. But before you create an investment strategy you've got to lay out some goals to reach and then create a timeline for reaching them. The goals should also be tailored to your personal financial situation. The key for good goal setting is to determine what your values are—to retire early, to travel the world, or to run your own small business—and then set about defining goals to help you meet those lifestyle values. Doing so makes it much easier to create a financial plan that works for you.

Chapter 2

THE REPORT CARD

"We may lose and we may win,
but we will never be here again."

— Jackson Browne

January 10, 2003

ROBIN SEWELL HUNG UP THE PHONE and cracked open her lap top computer. Clicking on an Excel spreadsheet file, she added a new client's name to her database—the third new client she'd gotten this month. "And it's not even the 15th yet," she thought.

With three new clients, Robin knew she'd need extra help. She called her assistant Raquel and asked her to bring in the "new résumés" file she'd been accumulating over the past few months. Thumbing through them, she pulled out the most promising ones and began emailing job candidates. "A graphic designer and an account exec, for sure," she thought. "Maybe a copywriter, too, although I can farm that one out I bet."

Patiently crafting her email queries, Robin contemplated how fast and how far her business had grown—and how fast and far she'd grown with it. She recalled eight years ago, with two young kids in grade school and the decision that she and Roy had made to hold off starting her business until the kids were older. At the time it was a gut-wrenching decision—they weren't exactly rolling in money. But the notion of staying home and raising her children was important to Robin. The business could wait.

Then, after that warm September morning when she bid Morgan goodbye for her first day of junior high, Robin got busy launching her new business. She'd been freelancing for a few months in preparation for the day when she'd hang out her own shingle but Robin knew that a few odd jobs here and there would be peanuts compared to running her own show, full time, six days a week.

Her fledgling public relations business had some trouble gaining traction, but, after a few tense moments and more than a few gray hairs waiting for checks and paying the bills for the computer and the other home office equipment she'd purchased down at Staples, things began ramping up quickly. After six months she had two full time clients and she was off and rolling. By the end of her first year she had four clients and had to hire her first employee. Now, eight years later, she had 23 clients and eight employees and her business was billing out $50,000 a month.

Robin started thinking about when she first started working on The Progression of Wealth. Her business was just a dream then and the information Jay and Brian had given the Sewells on their blueprint was still paying off for them. It had given Robin the confidence that, with the right financial plan, she could start her business. Back then she and Roy had struggled to balance the checkbook and she couldn't imagine running a successful business. However, Jay and Brian laid out a process called The Progression of Wealth for Business Owners that showed Robin exactly what she needed to do to start and run a successful business. Robin remembered when Jay told her, "If opening your own shop is part of your financial dream, then you have to have a plan to accommodate not just paying for your business, but accounting for the ripple effects that your business will have on your family finances." She thought back to that day eight years ago, when her present reality had just been a dream.

March 15, 1994 (eight years earlier)

Roy and Robin Sewell sat quietly in Jay Heller's office. Roy idly toyed with his car keys while Robin double-checked their binder that Brian reminded them to bring.

Jay came in from a meeting next door and exchanged pleasantries with the Sewells. Brian slid in a moment later. Heather walked in with some coffee. Jay thanked her and got right down to business.

Jay opened the meeting. "You know, guys, we've all heard the saying that nobody ever laid on their death bed regretting they should have spent more time in the office. It's the same idea with The Progression of Wealth Process. When your time comes you won't be regretting that you should have spent more time building wealth." Jay stopped to make sure he had their attention. Robin and Roy looked on attentively.

He continued. "Neither of you mentioned that was what you wanted when we went through The Progression of Wealth Blueprint." Jay reviewed the blueprint with the Sewells.

"Are you ready for The Report Card now?" asked Jay.

"Yep, as long as we don't have to get our parents to sign it," joked Roy.

"No you don't," said Jay, "but you might want to show it to Jack and Morgan so they can see that you don't get all A's all the time either."

"I think we'll just let them keep thinking we're perfect," said Robin.

Jay laughed. "Throughout your entire life you've been graded, in school, and now in your job through performance reviews. Most likely, you have given many grades yourself. We cannot escape receiving and giving grades. For example … 'That is a five star hotel,' 'Rated #1 in customer satisfaction,' 'That performance was a ten.' The list goes on and on."

Brian chimed in. "The one area, however, where most people never receive a grade is in the management of their wealth. Unfortunately, people will think if they got a 30% return in the stock market, they are doing a great job with their wealth. Our experience has revealed several weaknesses with just reviewing the performance of your investments to determine how you are doing. The first weakness is that most people don't know the performance of their entire portfolio. People remember the individual winners and the individual losers and if there are more winners than losers, they think things are good. Not knowing the annual performance of your portfolio is a fundamental problem hindering an honest assessment of the management of your wealth." He paused to sip some coffee. "In addition, not knowing the amount of risk you are taking with your investments is another problem. The second major weakness is that most people overestimate their ability to manage their wealth. These two weaknesses combined, not knowing and overestimating one's abilities, equal a recipe for trouble. Ignorance is bliss they say, but only until it's too late."

He paused to let it all sink in. "There are five areas that comprise wealth management," Brian added, counting them off on his fingers.

1. Liquidity/Cash Flow Management
2. Asset Growth
3. Leverage/Debt Management
4. Risk Management
5. Asset Protection

"Arguably there is a sixth category—Tax Management," he said. "We, however, have chosen to incorporate tax management throughout each of the five areas listed above. We believe taxes are integral to each area of wealth and to separate them into their own categories would undermine the importance of the effect taxes have on each area." Roy and Robin nodded.

"Through The Report Card we have assessed your performance on each of the five areas above. Here is a summary of your Report Card," said Brian, passing the Sewells some papers.

Roy and Robin Sewell

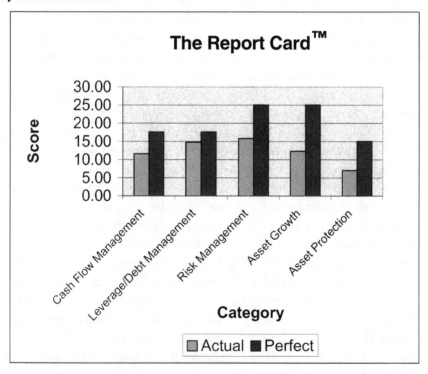

[See the Sewell's full Report Card in Appendix B on page 156.]

HJ Financial Group
The Report Card™

Category	Actual Score	Scoring Thresholds					Results	Comments
		A	B	C	D	F		
Cash Flow Management	Actual 11.55	Perfect 17.5	12 to 17	7 to 11	3 to 6	under 3	C	* A savings plan should be created to ensure you are maximizing your wealth accumulation ability.
Leverage/Debt Management	14.70	17.5	12 to 17	7 to 11	3 to 6	under 3	B	* Congratulations! You are using debt efficiently.
Risk Management	15.75	25	20 to 25	15 to 20	10 to 15	under 10	C	* You may be under insured in the case of a premature death. A comprehensive risk management program should be developed to ensure your family and your assets are protected.
Asset Growth	12.25	25	17 to 25	11 to 17	5 to 11	under 5	C	* An Investment Policy Statement should be developed to ensure that your asset allocation and risk level are appropriate to meet your goals.
Asset Protection	6.98	15	10 to 15	7 to 10	3 to 7	under 3	D	* Your Wills should be updated to ensure an orderly and tax efficient transfer of your wealth.

"The first area is liquidity or cash flow management," said Jay. "Why is liquidity important? Liquidity serves many important purposes. Liquidity prepares you for unexpected events like unanticipated expenses—you know, when the water heater breaks down or if you or your spouse suddenly become unemployed. Liquidity helps meet short-term commitments and obligations so that your long-term investments can continue to work for you. Cash Flow Management allows you to utilize your cash flows to balance your short-term liquidity needs with your long-term savings needs."

"Makes sense," said Roy. Robin nodded and sipped some coffee.

"The next area is Asset Growth," said Jay. "Asset Growth is the lifeline to your Financial Independence because the value of your assets will most likely dictate when you can retire and at what standard of living. We already mentioned that just looking at your portfolio return is not enough by itself."

"The next area is leverage/debt management." Brian picked up. "Debt in and of itself is neither good or bad. The management of the debt is what makes it either good or bad. But debt that has gotten out of control can have long-lasting adverse affects on your Financial Independence. It could lead to a poor credit history which in turn will affect your ability to access debt on favorable terms. It most certainly will affect your ability to save and will impact your liquidity.

"Risk management is the other side of asset growth. No one likes to buy insurance. Makes sense—it's just throwing good money down the drain. This is another area where most people overestimate themselves. Most people overestimate their own health and mortality. Everyone works so hard to get all the other areas working and simply ignores this area. Unfortunately you cannot ignore risk in hopes it will go away, because it won't. Risks must be identified and managed."

"The final area to score is asset protection," said Jay. "What good is it to expend all this effort to build your wealth only to have it taken away? This is another area similar to risk management that is often overlooked or flat out ignored. Asset Protection is the process of making sure that assets are available to you and your family regardless of unforeseen or uncontrollable events."

Robin looked closely at the paper in front of her. "I can't believe we got three Cs, a B, and a D. Are we that bad off?" she asked.

"Most of our clients are at the same point as you when they first come in," Jay assured them. "The Progression of Wealth Process will improve your scores almost immediately."

"Well I'm all for fast action," said Roy. "How do we get started?"

Jay smiled. "You already have. The Progression of Wealth Process will lead us the rest of the way."

Chapter Two Overview:
The Report Card™

The Report Card is a diagnostic tool that assesses and grades your Progression of Wealth to date. The Report Card is the first step in identifying the areas of your wealth that deserve the most attention. You will be scored in the areas of Cash Flow Management, Asset Growth, Leverage/Debt Management, Risk Management, and Asset Protection.

Chapter 3

THE FINANCIAL INDEPENDENCE CULTIVATOR

"You better start swimmin' or you'll sink like a stone,
'cause the times they are a-changin'."

– Bob Dylan

October 28, 1994

ROBIN LOOKED INTENTLY at the wooden cabinet door samples all around her. There were so many to choose from, all glistening newly from the store walls. She didn't know which she liked the best.

After she and Roy had kicked the can down the road on the matter for years, Robin knew that it was time to give the kitchen a face lift. They had lived in the house for years, and it was time to bring the kitchen up to speed. Rather than having the entire thing remodeled, she knew it was better to change the flooring and the cabinet faces. The appliances had been replaced recently enough that they still suited her needs. Now she wanted the rest of the place to look up to par.

"With you and Jack around, we certainly need to make sure our kitchen runs like a Swiss watch," she chided Roy, who was standing in front of a set of dark cabinet doors.

Roy ignored the barb. "What about these?" he asked, pointing.

Robin wrinkled her nose. "No, I think those are a bit too dark for my tastes. I want something lighter to open the room up."

Roy looked puzzled. "This is why I'm letting you handle this aspect of things, honey," he said. "I have absolutely no idea what you're talking about."

Robin smiled in satisfaction as she continued browsing. She had been fixing up the house little by little over the years. She loved the place, and was always finding ways to improve it to make it feel even more like home. Robin preferred doing this to moving. Their home was certainly more than just a house to them, so she was taking special care of it, and making it fit their needs exactly.

"Do you remember when all these renovations seemed out of our reach?" said Robin. "Before we'd started really managing our money?"

Roy nodded. "Yeah. We've come a long way in just a year. We didn't realize then what we know now: that it's best to save up some money and fix your house to be the way you want it to be instead of just moving somewhere else."

"Not only that, but we didn't even know the right way to save money before then," said Robin, stopping in front of a homey set of honey-colored cabinets. "Thank goodness we got our act together."

"Yep. Just in time, too," said Roy. "Speaking of kitchens, I'm starving. How about we go grab some lunch and continue this after we've got some fuel in our tummies?"

"Always thinking about food!" she scolded him teasingly.

April 22, 1994 (six months earlier)

"Are you sure you don't feel like therapists yet?" quipped Robin. She and Roy sat across from Jay and Brian in a booth at a local diner. They were meeting there for brunch rather than in the office.

"What do you mean?" asked Jay, lowering his menu.

Robin sighed. "We always come to you with our troubles. You must be starting to feel like we're in therapy."

Jay laughed. "That's what we're here for."

"As long as you don't start to reveal anything too twisted or Freudian," joked Brian.

"Ah, let's not go there!" said Roy, closing his menu and setting it down on the table.

"So," asked Jay, setting his own menu down. "Today we want to cover The Financial Independence Cultivator. This is the stage in which we turn your short-term goals into action and remove the psychological barriers that box most people in to The Fragmented Finances Trap that you were living in. How do you feel that things are coming along?"

"Good," said Robin, shifting in her seat. "I guess our biggest concerns today are worries about the future. For instance, there is so much we want to do to the house. Roy and I can't agree on how much we should spend renovating it."

Brian smiled. "Who doesn't worry about the future? I'd be worried if you *weren't* worried about the future. But once we hear your woes, I'm sure we can find a way to turn those worries into confidence."

"Are you sure you've got time for all these?" joked Roy. Just then a frazzled waitress appeared to take their order. Robin and Roy ordered omelets, Jay ordered pancakes and sausage, and Brian splurged on waffles.

"Considering how busy it is in here, I think we'll have more than enough time to hear what's on your minds," said Jay, taking a sip of water. "We might even be able to hear everything before she gets back here with the coffee."

"Well, I guess our main concerns are 'How will we retire? When can we retire? How will we be able to pay for the kids' college and still retire?' Those sorts of worries are the ones weighing heaviest on our minds at the moment," said Roy.

The waitress came back and clattered four coffee mugs onto the table. She hastily filled them with coffee before retreating to the kitchen.

Brian took a long sip. "Ah, that's better." He stirred more sugar into his cup before continuing. "The first thing I have to say is that it's a good thing that you're worrying about these sorts of things. Some people have the mindset of worrying about the future later—which doesn't really make any sense, if you think about it. The time to address things that may become a big concern in the future is in the present time, so that they don't become anything to worry about down the road."

"Makes sense," said Roy, pouring creamer into his coffee.

Robin fiddled with a packet of sugar. "I think the biggest problem is that we can't seem to save. At the end of the month there never is anything left for long-term savings."

Jay nodded. "And that's understandable. People usually tend to prioritize their short-term goals because they see the results a lot more quickly and get to experience the rewards sooner. This is the instant gratification syndrome that's become such a trend in this country. The problem with doing that is if you don't do anything towards accomplishing long-term goals, you're going to run into problems in the future—especially when your long-term goals involve your finances."

"Which ours do," said Robin.

"We've developed something to help people achieve those long-term goals using a short-term mindset," said Brian. "It's called The Financial Independence Cultivator. We've developed this because the decisions you make today will have a profound impact on your future."

"Let's face it," Jay picked up, "when short-term goals compete with long-term goals, the short-term ones will win out. That's where The Financial Independence Cultivator comes in."

"What is it, exactly?" asked Roy, draining his coffee cup.

"The Financial Independence Cultivator is a way to coordinate your goals and develop a strategy so that both your short-term and long-term goals are working together," Jay explained. "Not only will they be working together, but your short-term goals will be assisting you in meeting your long-term goals. Perfect harmony—that's what The Financial Independence Cultivator gives you."

"Sounds good to me," said Roy. "That's certainly a concept: making short-term goals work in our favor."

"That sounds like just what we need," said Robin.

Just then the waitress appeared with their plates. She slid them onto the table, then rushed off to get them more coffee.

"Ah," said Roy, rubbing his hands together over his plate. "Can't wait to dig in."

"Well, you go ahead and we'll explain things a bit," said Brian.

"Consider it done," said Roy, loading his fork with home fries.

"Think back to your blueprint," said Jay, spreading jelly on his toast. "We helped you create a vision of your future, in the next year and through the next five years. What is your plan to achieve these? By achieving these goals, are you sacrificing other goals? It is a delicate balance to allow yourself the opportunity to meet all your goals." Roy nodded.

"I think it would be best to start with five basic myths that seriously influence most people's short-term approach to their finances," said Brian, setting down his coffee cup. These misconceptions force people to live in The Fragmented Finances Trap." He began ticking off the reasons on his fingers. "First off, people believe that having any debt is bad. Second, and related to this, is the belief that paying off your mortgage early is great because you build up equity faster. Third is that investing in real estate, especially in your house, always pays off. Fourth is that you can pay for things today out of your salary and make up savings later through bonuses and pay raises. And the fifth is that the stock market is too risky."

"I was always a fan of mythology in my college literature classes, but I'm not sure I like the sounds of these myths," said Robin.

"Me either," smiled Jay. "But, if we can change your mind about how you think of the five myths we mentioned, then we will be able to help you meet your long-term goals. We'll be able to show you how to use the Financial Independence Cultivator as a powerful tool to harmonize your short-term and long-term goals."

"I'm no musician, but this harmony sounds like something I could really get into," said Roy, finishing a piece of toast.

"Great," said Brian. "Let's start with the first myth that debt is bad. On the surface, this seems like a sound concept. But what exactly is debt? It's borrowing money from someone today with the obligation to repay the money later. The catch is that you have to pay them interest to be able to use the money today."

"That's never a pleasant thought," said Roy. He stabbed a piece of omelet with his fork.

"But, unlike what's written in the Constitution that all men are created equal, *not* all debt is created equal," Jay said. "There is bad debt and good debt. Examples of bad debt are credit card debt, certain leases or automobile loans, personal loans, and consolidation loans."

Now it was Robin's turn. "Ooh, credit card debt. The thought of that makes my stomach turn."

"Lay off the shopping sprees at Macy's," Roy teased her.

"The one thing these debts all have in common is a high rate of interest," Jay continued. "None of them start out that way, and that's how they hook you, but after the introductory period expires the rates increase significantly. This is known as the 'teaser rate'."

"Nobody likes a tease," quipped Roy.

"The teaser rate entices you into consolidating debt, or transferring balances in the search of a great deal. Unfortunately, that great deal doesn't exist out there in the land of bad debt," said Brian.

"Figures," said Roy.

"Credit card debt is always bad unless you pay off the balance each month," Brian continued. "So we advocate always paying off your credit card balance each month, regardless of the current interest rate on the card. Credit cards should be used as a convenience of not having to carry cash with you."

"You should take notes on this, honey," said Roy, elbowing Robin in the ribs.

"Oh, like you never use credit cards!" she snorted. "Need I remind you of the Radio Shack credit card you nearly melted from use last month?"

Jay smiled. "If you get into the habit of always paying off your credit card balances each month, you will never fall victim to the trap of just paying the required minimum payment because it is low. Don't tell yourself, 'Oh, I'll just pay this amount until some additional cash comes in.' The point is that if you can't afford it today, you most likely won't be able to afford it tomorrow."

Roy thought about this, then nodded. "Good point. Looks like we've got to tighten the reins on the credit card usage."

"The other loans generally fall into the same trap," said Brian. Then there's the question of leasing. Ah, yes, the lease versus buying question. Which makes the most sense? While the answer tends to be based on your personal circumstances, there are some general rules of thumb. First off, if you plan on owning the car longer than 5 years, or if you know you will put more miles on the car than the lease allows, then buying will be the better answer. But, if you like the look, feel, and smell of a new car every 3-4 years and your normal commute to work is predictable, leasing will be the better answer."

"Gotta love that new car smell," said Roy. "But that certainly does make sense. We've been thinking that it's about time to get a new car, so this is good advice."

"But here's a word to the wise," Brian cautioned. "Don't lease your car only to purchase it through financing when it is about to come off the lease. The residual or buy-out of the leases are too expensive, and basically you're financing the car twice: first during the initial lease term and second when the car comes off the lease. You would be better off buying the car up front."

"Who knew the car buying process was this in-depth?" said Robin, finishing her orange juice.

"As far as buying is concerned, the Internet is a wonderful tool to tell you what the dealer paid for the car and what you should expect to pay," said Jay. "Another rule of thumb is that you are usually better off negotiating the price of the car, taking the manufacturer's rebates, and arranging your own bank financing. Taking the dealer's low rate for financing will limit your ability, as well as their desire, to negotiate a better price. In the end, you'll just be overpaying for the car."

"This is all good stuff to know," said Roy.

"You had mentioned that there's such a thing as good debt," said Robin. "What's that about? How can debt be good?"

"You need to think like a CEO or business owner for a minute," said Brian. "Would you think that a company with no debt is a good thing? Probably not! As a business owner, you have several decisions you can make with the operating revenue of your company. You could use the revenue to reinvest it back into the company's operations. You could use the revenue to pay your shareholders dividends. You could buy back your stock, or you could pay down your debt."

"Well, this is good info to know too," said Robin, "since I'm thinking of starting my own business sometime soon. But which of the choices you just mentioned is the right one?"

"Well that depends," said Brian. "It depends on the opportunity cost of the option you're not choosing. For example, let's say a company's historical return on equity, or ROE, has been 10% and management feels that it can sustain this ROE into the future. If their current debt is at 7%, wouldn't the company be better reinvesting the revenue in their operation versus paying down their debt? After all, the opportunity cost is 3% better in the company."

"So to answer the question of how can there be good debt, simply rephrase it to, 'Is there a better opportunity to use the money elsewhere?'" Jay explained. "To truly be able to answer this question, you must believe that the long-term returns of the stock market outperform all other asset classes. If you believe this then the answer is simple. If you don't believe this, then The Investment Portfolio Optimizer will prove this to you."

"Convinced?" asked Brian. Robin and Roy nodded. "Good. So good debt is any debt that has a lower interest rate than the annual average return for the stock market over the long term—meaning 10 to 12%. For example, consider the current interest rate on your home. Mortgage debt is usually 'good debt,' especially in this interest rate environment. Prime rate is 6.00%[3]. Thirty year mortgages are around 7.5%[3]."

"Speaking of which, wasn't one of the myths about paying our mortgage?" asked Robin.

---

3. In 2003 The Prime Interest Rate was 4.25% and the average 30-year mortgage rate was 5.5%.

"Yes," said Jay. "The second myth is that paying off your mortgage early is great because you're building up equity faster."

"If you can invest your money in the stock market and get 10 to 12% in returns, why would you be apt to pay down your debt at 7.5% ?" Brian chimed in. "Because there are no guarantees in the stock market right? Wrong. This is something you have to trust me on. And it will become clearer to you once we go over The Investment Portfolio Optimizer with you."

Roy nodded. "Okay. For the sake of argument, let's say we accept it. Then what?"

"Well," said Brian, signaling to the waitress. "Once you've mastered this concept, which you just claimed to have done, you're already well ahead of your friends and neighbors and are well on your way to financial independence. Ask yourself, 'What do the big financial service companies know that they don't want me to know?' It's simple: they know the 'law of averages' and the long-term prospects of the stock market. Why else would a bank or insurance company be willing to guarantee you 5 or 6% on your money so long as you agree to keep it with them for 5 to 10 years? It's because they're going to take your money, invest it in the stock market, earn 10 to 12% and pay you 5 to 6%. Remember, they're in the business to make money for their owners and shareholders."

The waitress finally arrived at their table, and Brian asked for more coffee. She hurried away to get it.

"Now for the best news of all," said Jay.

"Great, I'd like to hear some good news," said Roy, eating his last bite of home fries.

"You get an income tax deduction for the mortgage interest you pay."

"Really!" exclaimed Robin. "I didn't know that."

"That's right," Jay continued, pushing his coffee cup towards the waitress, who had just returned with the coffee. "Your 'good debt' just got better. For example, if we were to look at the difference of growth of 10% versus 7.5% , you can have substantially more money by not paying down your debt early. With the income tax deduction, your effective borrowing rate is 4.88%, assuming a 35% effective tax rate."

"This flies in the face of conventional wisdom and most people's comfort level," said Brian, nodding as the waitress departed. "Implementing this concept isn't easy, but you will be rewarded in the long run. There are certainly benefits to building up equity in your home. The main benefit is the ability to access the equity so you can borrow more. So if you are averse to debt—why are you in a hurry to pay down that mortgage?"

"Guess we're not," said Robin.

"There's even more on good debt," said Jay. "A Home Equity Line of Credit is a great source of liquidity. We just spent a long time explaining to you about good debt," said Jay. "But by no means are we advocating living beyond your means through debt. This seems to be the American way: why pay to-day what you can pay for twice in the future? So it is with great caution that we recommend this concept. You have to be especially careful if you have a bad track record with debt management, because then the Home Equity Line of Credit is not for you and you could be jeopardizing your home."

"But now for the benefits of the Home Equity Line of Credit, or HELOC," said Brian. "The HELOC is a line of credit available for you to borrow against. The key difference is that it's available to you and you don't pay a penny in interest or fees until you actually use the HELOC. To get the most favorable outcome, you generally do not want to borrow more than 80% of the value of your home. This is the loan to value ratio, or LTV ratio. Here is how to calculate it." Brian took a pen from his pocket and grabbed a napkin. Roy and Robin leaned in closer to look.

"Let's say the current market value of your home is $250,000 and your out-standing loan balance is $125,000. Then the current LTV ratio is 50%. So to take your LTV ratio up to 80%, you can take a HELOC for $75,000 and still get the best rate and terms. And fortunately, the interest is tax deductible." Brian put away his pen.

"In a nutshell, what we're revealing here is a strategy that most, if not all, highly successful business owners, attorneys, CPAs and other professionals use," said Jay. "They live off their modest base salary and utilize their HE-LOC to fund their ongoing cash flow needs. This is how they supplement their salaries until their guaranteed payments are paid out at the end of the year. But keep in mind that I said *guaranteed* payments. These professionals are not living beyond their means, they are simply supplementing their cash flow through their HELOC. Once they receive their guaranteed payments, they will pay back their HELOC."

"Gotcha," said Roy. "What about the real estate investment myth?"

"Your house is somewhere you live, and it generally will appreciate over the years," Brian explained. "You shouldn't consider your house an invest-ment that you will rely on for retirement and other major goals. And unless

Loan-To-Value (LTV)

Current Home Value (HV) = $250,000
Current Loan Balance (LB) = $125,000

$$LTV = \frac{LB}{HV} = \frac{125,000}{250,000} = 50\%$$

If you want your LTV = 80%, then:

$$80\% = \frac{x}{250,000} = \$200,000 \text{ Loan Balance}$$

So your HELOC can be up to:

$$\$200,000 - \$125,000 = \underline{\$75,000}$$

you are willing to sell your house when the real estate market appreciates and wait a few years until you can find a similar house cheaper—or better yet, downsize—you will not realize the gains from selling your home."

"Ouch," said Robin.

"Most people do the opposite," Brian continued. "They sell their house only to move to a more expensive area or a bigger home. I recognize that your house is the biggest investment you will make in your life but you have to recognize what it is. It's where you're going to live, eat, sleep, raise your children, and share memories. It isn't something that you are actively look-ing to sell at the right price. Vacation homes fall into the same category. You use them for enjoyment and generally are not looking to sell them in the short term for a profit."

"Real estate investing is a full time job done by qualified real estate profes-sionals. These professionals know how to identify a great property and then use other people's money to buy it and sell it quickly for a profit, and they do this over and over again. Or alternatively, they need to be a landlord who regularly collects rent and has their properties fully leased nearly all the time," Jay explained.

"What you should do instead is buy a house to live in that you can truly afford," said Brian. "By afford, we mean that you can afford the monthly payment, taxes, and insurance and still have the ability to save in your retirement accounts and other investments. So many people become house rich and cash poor. This limits their ability to ever save until the kids are out of college. By then, retirement is near and there is little time to play catch up."

"The next myth is that you can pay for things today out of your salary and make up the savings later through bonuses and pay raises," said Jay. "This rarely happens, so get the idea out of your head immediately. So many people continue to put money into their house each year trying to make it perfect. Most people have a never-ending list of improvements they want to make to their home or lawn or whatever."

"For us it's the kitchen," said Robin, giving Roy a look.

"The problem, as I'm sure you know, is that these projects get funded out of current income and then you have to raid the savings accounts to pay off the credit card balance. While I agree with paying off your whole credit card balance, the problem is putting off your savings plan, or worse yet, raiding your existing savings, which sets you back years on retirement."

This has to do with the simple concept of compounding." Brian picked up where Jay had left off. "When the earnings you make on your original investment grow, your money is compounding. A rule of thumb is if you earn 7% on your money, over time your money will double every 10 years. Compounding takes time and when you continue to postpone your savings you lose one of the most valuable asset you have—time! And you can't get time back."

"They always say that time is money," said Roy.

"Exactly," Jay agreed. "So what we suggest doing is establishing systematic monthly savings programs for your taxable accounts, just like you have for your 401(k) accounts. What this means is that you pay yourself first. If you get into this habit, you won't miss the money after a few months. Even if you do, do everything you can to avoid touching it. Make it hard to get to."

"Sounds like just what we need to do, honey," said Robin. Roy nodded.

"The last myth that we're here to dispel is that the stock market is too risky an option," said Brian. "Many people think that you should only put money you can afford to lose into the stock market because it is a big gamble. They think you'd be better off going to Las Vegas and putting it on the roulette table."

"And while Vegas might be a blast, this isn't a good way of looking at things," said Jay. "Usually the people saying things like this are those who have accumulated no wealth. But you have to ask yourself who invests in the stock market and then take a look at the wealthiest families in America. The Rockefellers. The Vanderbilts. The Mellons. The Astors. A significant amount of their wealth is in the stock market. Did any of these people make their money gambling? No, but they were willing to take risks that they could control and over time wound up ahead."

"The stock market doesn't have to be a risky venture," said Brian. "Think about this: how are wealthy families investing? On their own or through a team of professional financial and investment advisors? I think it's safe to say that you know the answer to this one. So take a lesson from these families. Having at least some money allocated to the stock market is a good thing."

"Basically, we say that 'TIME AND DIVERSIFICATION' work in stock market investing," explained Jay. "You first need to understand your goals and the amount needed to fund these goals. Then you develop an Investment Policy Statement that addresses your goals, time horizon and risk tolerance. Then you develop an asset allocation that will allow you to achieve the return you need to accomplish your goals. And finally, hire professional money managers to manage the money through a diversified investment portfolio. We'll talk a little bit more about this in future meetings. We just want to be sure you realize that the stock market is not a gamble and that over a longer time period it becomes close to a sure thing."

"This makes sense, too," said Roy. "This has really opened up my mind."

The waitress came to clear their plates and drop off the check. Brian snatched it up. "Let us treat you this time," he said.

"But you've already done more than enough to help us," protested Robin.

"Next time we go out to get brunch, it can be on you, how's that?" Brian asked.

"Deal," said Robin.

Jay leaned back in his seat and took his final sip of coffee. "So let's run down the steps we went over today on how you can take action immediately to begin cultivating your financial independence. First, pay off your credit card balances every month. Second, if you have equity on your home, establish a home equity line of credit. Third, make sure that your house is one you love and can easily afford. Fourth, establish a monthly systematic savings program right out of your checking account, so that you won't dip into retirement money. And finally, invest that monthly savings into a diversified investment portfolio that is appropriate to you and your particular situation."

"Wow, sounds like we went over quite a lot today," said Roy. "It amazes me that you guys remember this all."

"It's the years of practice at doing it," said Brian.

"But just in case your memories aren't entirely photographic, here is a copy of The Financial Independence Cultivator for your binder. We have included an Action Plan so we can easily track your progress," Jay assured them.

"Terrific," said Robin. "I know that it will be helpful for me to have something to go over later at home. And with him"—she jerked her thumb at Roy—"he forgets everything the moment he hears it!"

"What, honey?" he asked, looking over at her.

"Exactly my point!" Robin exclaimed.

Chapter 3 Overview:
Financial Independence Cultivator™

The purpose of the Financial Independence Cultivator is to develop a specific action plan that will allow you to meet all your short-term goals, which are the goals you want to achieve within the next five years.

TAKE ACTION NOW *to begin to cultivate your path to financial independence. You can dispel each of the 5 myths we discussed by implementing the 5 concepts below. Implement them today and you will be securing your financial independence tomorrow.*

- *Pay off all your credit cards every month.*
- *If you have equity on your home, establish a home equity line of credit for liquidity purposes.*
- *Buy a house you love and can easily afford.*
- *Establish a monthly systematic savings program right out of your checking account.*
- *Invest that monthly savings into a diversified investment portfolio that is appropriate for you.*

Chapter 4

THE INVESTMENT PORTFOLIO OPTIMIZER

"A new day will dawn for those who stand strong,
and the forests will echo with laughter."
– R. Plant/ J. Page

May 1, 1998

JACK SEWELL WAS OFF AT THE CRACK OF THE BAT. Positioned in deep center with the clean-up hitter at the plate, Jack sprinted toward the gap between left and center fields, gauging the flight of the fly ball while keeping one eye on the green outfield fence that was drawing closer by the moment. Finally, as he felt the gravel of the warning track crunching underfoot, Jack leapt at the wall and snared the ball in the web of his glove. Bracing himself, Jack landed at the foot of the fence, using his free hand to steady himself against the wall as his feet hit the ground. "Whew," he thought. "Nearly missed that one."

Tony Banks, the left fielder for The Shipley School Gators, sprinted over to Jack. "Dude! Great catch! You okay?"

Jack nodded his head and threw the ball back to the infield. He barely noticed the crowd rising to its feet to applaud the fine play. "Two out, right, Tee?"

Tony nodded back. "Yeah, that's two. One more and we're in the play-offs. So don't get all high and mighty on me. The next guy's liable to hit one outta here, too." He sprinted back to his position in left, while Jack ran back to his position in center field.

250 feet away, still clapping, stood Roy, Robin, and Morgan Sewell. They had come out to cheer Jack on a gorgeous May afternoon, one in which The Shipley School baseball team hoped to capture a berth in the playoffs. A win today over neighboring Germantown Academy would do the trick. So far, so good. The Gators clung to a one-run lead in the bottom of the seventh—and last—inning. "Oh Roy! Did you see that catch!" Robin shouted, beaming with pride. "That was a gem!"

Roy settled back into his lawn chair. "It was great alright. He must get that sprinter's speed from my side of the family."

Robin dug an elbow into his shoulder. "Hey, I'm the runner in this family. He obviously got it from me." Morgan chuckled as Robin waved over to Marisa Banks and gave her a big thumbs-up. Marisa held up her index finger, silently mouthing the words "one more to go."

The next hitter, on a two-and-one count, swung and lofted a lazy fly ball to left field. "Can o' Corn!" Roy shouted, leaping back to his feet. "C'mon Tony, get under it!"

Tony Banks glided effortlessly under the ball, shading his eyes from the sun. Squeezing the ball tightly in his glove, he leapt into the air, pumping his fist. The Gators were in.

Bedlam ensued on the field. Parents, students, teachers, and players converged on the infield diamond. Players thumped each other on the back. Coach Reilly yelled over to Jack "Great catch, Jack! Just great!"

Robin Sewell raced toward Jack and gave him a hug. "Jeez, Mom, not now," he said, eyeing his teammates, many of whom were fending off hugs from their own parents. Morgan hung back a bit, smiling and eyeballing the other boys on the team. Roy looked on proudly. Jack noticed and pulled himself away from the scrum. He walked over to Roy and gave him a high-five. "Good job, Jack. For a second there, I didn't think you'd run that last one down."

Jack smiled, glad that he had his Dad's approval. "Never a doubt, big guy. Never a doubt." Jack patted him on the back.

"Go on ahead, we'll catch up with you later," said Roy. "Right now I have to get your sister away from those boys. And I think there's a big party somewhere downtown tonight that you'll want to be going to." He pointed a finger at Jack. "Keep your head straight, though. Don't you and your friends do anything to jeopardize the play-offs now. They start on Monday, you know."

"I won't, Dad," Jack replied, already running back to his teammates. "Catch you later."

Winding down from a round of high-fives of her own, Robin broke away from the pack and walked back to where Roy was folding the lawn chairs and closing up the cooler. "Hey Hon, I invited the Banks over to celebrate. Told the Steins and O'Neils to come, too." She grabbed his arm as they headed off to the car.

"That's fine," Roy said, somewhat absent-mindedly.

"What's wrong, Hon?" Robin asked.

He stayed silent for a moment. "Well, for the first time, I'm starting to think that Jack might be far along enough where he might compete for a scholarship. He's got the grades and, from what I've seen this season, he's got the game to compete at the Division I college level. Heck, any team would love to have a kid who can hit and run a ball down in the alley like he can."

"You think?"

"I do, I really do," he replied.

Robin thought on it for a moment. "Well, the important thing is that, scholarship or not, two years from now he'll be going to college—and a good one at that. We've taken care of that, haven't we?"

"Yeah," said Roy. "Yeah, we have. But a scholarship to Arizona State or Wake Forest. Can you imagine that!"

Robin shook her head. "Hey, four years ago I couldn't imagine that we'd have the money to send him anywhere. Same for Morgan. But we do now. We do now."

Morgan had sidled up and heard the tail end of the conversation. "As long as the school has some cute boys," she grinned.

May 5, 1994 (four years earlier)

Brian shuffled some documents into an orderly pile and leaned back in his chair.

Sitting across from him were Roy and Robin Sewell. At his left was Jay Heller, sipping on a bottle of spring water.

Robin cleared her throat. "We had some great meetings so far. Roy and I are really encouraged."

Roy nodded. "Yeah, I figured that since I watch CNBC and read The Wall Street Journal once or twice a week, there really wasn't much about investing that I didn't already know."

"That's right," Robin added. "We've been managing our own money for a while now. It never occurred to us to actually pay anyone to do this for us."

"Turns out there's a bit more to it than that," Jay said, putting his water bottle back down on the table. "You guys ever hear of an investment policy statement?"

"Well, if you mean do we have anything that we put down in writing—no, we don't," Roy answered.

Jay jotted something down on a notepad. "Okay. Let me ask you this. Do you know what the performance of your investment portfolio was last year?"

Roy looked at Robin. She shrugged her shoulders. "I think we did better than most people," she said. "Definitely better than the stock market. We diversified with some no-load mutual funds. And we have a lot of international funds, especially emerging markets. Some of our funds were up over 80% in 1993."

Jay wrote that down, too. He put the pen back down on the conference table. Brian rolled his eyes—he felt a story coming.

"There was this guy—a rich guy—by the name of Jay Gould," said Jay. "A big financier in his day, Gould was known as "The Devil of Wall Street for his uncanny ways of being on the right side of a stock at the right time. One Sunday, Gould found himself greeting his minister after church. After exchanging pleasantries, the minister mentioned that the church had recently received $20,000 in donations and asked Gould whether he had any hot tips on the market. "Sure," Gould said. "Invest the money in Missouri Pacific". Sure enough, the minister did just that. Happily he watched the stock rise for several weeks. Unhappily, he watched it crash for weeks after. The minister mentioned the bad news to Gould. Lickety-split, Gould wrote a check for the full $20,000 right on the spot. Relieved, but anxious, the minister added that he'd given the tip to many members of his congregation. "No problem," Gould answered. "They were the ones I was after all along."

Roy smiled. "Good story. But are we the minister or are we the congregation?"

Jay smiled back. "Not important—for now. The point I want you to remember is that while the minister lucked out in the long run, he learned a painful lesson on the importance of investment risk. What I want you to take away from this story is that you always must know going in what you can afford to lose and, going forward, manage your portfolio correspondingly."

Brian looked up from his notes. "That's right. The higher the potential return, the greater the investment risk. That's a big rule on Wall Street."

"Define risk for us," Robin said, leaning forward in her seat.

"I'll take this one," Jay said, glancing at Brian. "When it comes to investing your money, it's critical. If establishing goals and having a plan is the foundation for your portfolio plan, then risk, along with diversification, is the framework. While risk is based primarily on your comfort level, it's also based on your ever-changing financial picture, your need for cash, investment preferences, time horizon, and other factors. Knowing your risk tolerance level is a critical factor if you're to build a dynamite portfolio, as it helps determine what kinds of investments best accommodate your investment goals."

He took another sip of water. "That said, risk can mean different things to different people. At the high end, fooling around with risk can lead to economic disaster. That's what investors of real estate deals learned in the 1980s.

"Yeah, that was a shame what happened to those people in the stock market in 1987," Robin said. "Still, how do you define risk so something like that doesn't happen to us?"

Brian jumped in. "Economists and most stock market experts define risk as the variance in return that is created by market volatility. In plain English, what they're saying is that your stocks will, given time, move up and down. It's the "up and down" part that really concerns those of us who build investment portfolios."

"That's right," Jay added. "You see, volatility—the up and down thing—can wreak havoc on your portfolio's performance. But you have to live with some volatility over the long term. Things are going to go up and down and you have to expect that—especially if you take on more risk."

Asset Class Performance: Risk/Reward Ratio

In Jay and Brian's discussion of the long-term performance of the investment markets, they discussed the risk-return trade off between protecting

The Progression of Wealth™

HJ Financial Group
Certified Public Accountants
Business and Personal Financial Advisors

RISK

Safety of Principal
Reduced Potential for Return

Increased Risk
Increased Potential for Return

	Principal Safety	Income	Income / Growth	Growth	AggressiveGrowth
Minimum Holding Period	None Immediate Liquidity	2 Years – 5 Years	4 Years – 7 Years+	5 Years – 10 Years +	10 Years – 15 Years +
Asset Allocation	_____ % $ _____	_____ % $ _____	_____ % $ _____	_____ % $ _____	_____ % $ _____
Potential Annual Market Risk	Guarantee of Principal	Conservative risk with relatively low principal fluctuation	Low to moderate risk with moderate principal fluctuation and income as downside protection	Moderate risk with substantial principal fluctuation	Aggressive risk with very substantial principal fluctuation
Typical Investment Alternatives	CDs* Money markets Passbook Savings* High Rated Commercial Paper Guaranteed Account	Treasury Bills & Notes Short- to Intermediate- Term Bonds / Bond Funds • Municipal • Corporate • Government • GNMA Utilities / Funds	Treasury Bonds Balanced Funds Equity Income Funds Long-term Bond Funds	Real Estate LP Long-term Bond Funds Stocks / Stock Funds • Blue chips • S&P 500 Index Limited Partnerships Multi-market Trust	Real Estate (leveraged) Stocks / Stock Funds • Sector • OTC – small cap • Foreign
Historical Long-Term Return	2 – 4%	4 – 6%	6 – 8%	8 – 10%	10 – 12%

This chart illustrates the relative differences among various investments, including potential risk of principal, ideal holding period, and general investment objectives among these categories. Holding period refers to the minimum time generally considered to be required to potentially achieve a positive rate of return while potentially reducing the average annual volatility of the investment.

* Bank accounts and CDs are insured by the FDIC.

Note: The Annualized Return History above is based on historical asset class returns using a variety of market indicators, including, among others, the following indicators: U.S. stocks – S&P 500 Index; Ibbotson U.S. Small Cap: Developed International stocks – MSCI EAFE Index; Emerging Markets Equity – IFC Investable Index; U.S. Bonds – U.S. Intermediate-Term Government, U.S. Short-Term Government, U.S. Long-Term Government, Lehman 3–10 Year Index; U.S. Long-Term Corporates; Mortgages – NAREIT; International Bonds – Salomon WGBI Index; High Yield Bonds – CSFB High Yield Index; Emerging Markets Debt – J.P. Morgan EMBI+; Fixed Annuities – U.S. Long-Term Corporates; Real Estate – Real Estate Composite; Cash – Ibbotson 30 Day T-Bill. Individual assets and asset allocation portfolios may perform better or worse than the representative asset class indicated.

HJ Financial, Suite H-1, 1000 Germantown Pike, Plymouth Meeting, PA 19462 ˉ Phone (610) 272 - 4700   Fax (610) 272 - 6785 ˉ   www.hjfinancialgroup.com

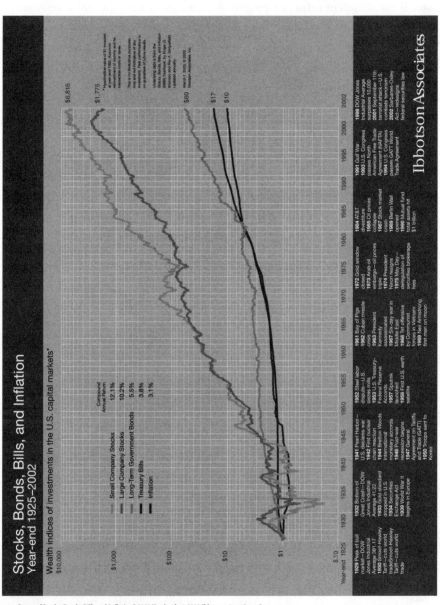

Stocks, Bonds, Bills, and Inflation
Year-end 1925–2002

Wealth indices of investments in the U.S. capital markets*

	Compound Annual Return
Small Company Stocks	12.1%
Large Company Stocks	10.2%
Long-Term Government Bonds	5.5%
Treasury Bills	3.8%
Inflation	3.1%

$6,816
$1,775
$60
$17
$10

Ibbotson Associates

your portfolio and growing your portfolio. Jay pulled out a worksheet that had "Risk Profile – Investment Alternatives" at the top and discussed with the Sewells the different returns that can be expected from different investments and the risks associated with those returns. Jay wrote the range of returns on the worksheet as he discussed each one. *(See worksheet on page 62.)*

"Look, there is no question—the historical evidence bears this out—that the more emphasis you place on stocks in your portfolio, the better your investments will do," said Brian. Jay pulled out a chart that showed the historical returns of the stock market and other asset classes from 1925 to present and discussed it with the Sewells. *(See page 63.)*

Jay nodded. "While we, as a rule of thumb, never use more than 10% annual returns on stocks in our client's portfolio projections, we do think that stocks are the best way to create wealth."

Roy interjected. "Does HJ Financial Group have an investment philosophy?"

"We sure do," Jay said. "We base our entire investment process on the foundation Nobel Prize economist Harry Markowicz developed, that asset allocation accounts for over 90% of investment returns. But unfortunately, most people spend all their efforts on the 10% of which stocks or funds to buy and hardly any time on asset allocation."

"Wow. Guilty as charged," Roy said.

"But Roy is doing fine with his stock picking so far," said Robin.

Brian broke into a grin. "That's great. You and the rest of the world." He took out his notepad and showed it to the Sewells. "Much of what we are talking about has to do with a term economists call 'standard deviation'." He flipped a page and drew a bell curve on it.

"Oh boy. I slept through this class at college," Roy said.

"It's not so bad," Brian replied. "Look what I've done here with your portfolio."

Brian used a 10% expected return and the historical volatility of the S&P 500 (19% over the previous 3 years). He showed the Sewells that the expected range of returns of the S&P 500 was between +48% and −28%. Then he showed them that there was a 95% probability that the S&P 500 would be between these numbers over any three-year period with the average being around 10%.

"That may seem like a pretty wide range to you," Brian continued, concluding that the standard deviation rate that he was formulating for the Sewells was 28%.

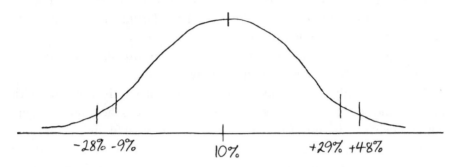

At 2 Standard Deviations there is a 95% probability that the Return will be between -28% and +48%.

At 1 Standard Deviation there is a 66% probability that the Return will be between -9% and +29%.

"What we're saying," Jay said, "is that if your portfolio loss is 25% you need a 50% return to get back to the high."

"Ouch," Roy said. "That hurts." They had his attention now. "What else can you tell us about our portfolio?"

"Well you have a large concentration of stock in your company, which accounts for about 40% of your total portfolio," Brian said. "You participate in your firm's ESOP Plan, have stock in your 401(k) Plan and you also get stock options. All that has resulted in the large standard deviation in your portfolio."

"Granted," said Roy. "But I know my company better than any other investment I own."

"True," Jay said. "But remember when Donald Trump had all his assets tied up in commercial real estate when the market went south and he filed for bankruptcy? Mr. Trump set himself up for a steep fall by putting all his eggs in one basket. Lack of diversification has a long history of wreaking havoc on people's wealth."

"The other problem is that you have such a low cost basis in the stock options that you will have a tax problem when you exercise your options," said Brian. "You have to be very careful how you exercise your stock options and what you do with the stock. We also want you to recognize that holding so much in your company stock increases the overall risk in your portfolio because the performance of the portfolio will be so heavily influenced by the performance of your company stock."

Robin jumped in. "With all due respect, we're not stupid. We do diversify our portfolio with different mutual fund investments."

"That is certainly the right idea," said Jay. "But one of the problems with mutual funds is that you don't know exactly what stocks the fund managers buy and in what amounts. Unfortunately, a lot of mutual funds buy the same stocks. We call this 'portfolio overlap.' We ran a portfolio overlap report for your investments and here is what we found." Jay showed the Sewells a Powerpoint chart:

Sewell's Stock Overlap Report

- 5 of 7 of the funds hold your company stock, thus further increasing your concentration of the stock to 45%,
- All 7 of the funds hold 52 of the same stocks,
- 85% of your portfolio is concentrated in 10 stocks.

"Yikes", said Roy. "I thought we were much more diversified than that. But how would you control that when you really don't know what these funds buy. Plus, these funds have good long-term track records so they must be doing something right."

"Sure, said Brian. "You don't know what these funds buy and all you have to go on is the long-term track record. However, what the overlap report shows you is you have a lot more risk in your portfolio than you thought you did. That's why your portfolio has such a large standard deviation. This has been rewarding in this bull market, but if and when we go into a bear market your portfolio will be in trouble."

"Light bulb time," said Roy, shaking his head.

"No worries," Jay said. "We're going to help you." He picked up another document.

"One last observation we have for your portfolio is a concept called "style drift". Familiar with the term?"

Robin looked at Roy. "No, not exactly," she answered.

"That's okay," Brian said. "Style drift is when a mutual fund changes its stripes and begins investing in a hot part of the market. The manager is trying to chase returns because the fund's style of investment is currently out of favor with the market. For example, what has been the hot part of the market for the past two years?"

"That's easy," said Roy. "International stocks and emerging markets companies."

"Yep," said Jay. "And what about growth versus value stocks?"

"Value stocks were much hotter," said Robin.

"Yes," said Jay. "To be specific, small company stocks and emerging market companies were the place to invest in 1992 and 1993. But that ended in 1994 when international stocks of developed countries were on top and large cap growth stocks outperformed large cap value stocks. So things change. Sometimes quickly." Jay pulled out another chart that showed the Asset Class Returns from 1981 to present to bring the point home that it is nearly impossible to accurately guess which part of the stock market will be on top from year to year. *(See page 68.)*

"Gotcha," said Roy. "What about our mutual funds?"

Jay rummaged through the pile for the right document. "When you look at the overlap report, you see a lot of your funds buying the same stocks but when you look at the reported investment style of the fund, some are value managers and some are growth managers. We took a look at a style analysis of your managers on a year by year basis and studied the results. Only two of your managers have stuck with their investment style over the past 10 years. The other five funds have changed their investment style at least three times over the past 10 years."

Robin looked puzzled. "Don't you want a fund manager who changes his style to invest in stocks that are on the rise?"

"Well, yes and no," said Brian. "You want your managers to invest in stocks that will go up within their reported investment style. Let's say you entered the stock market in 1988 and decided half of your money should be in growth stocks and half your money should be in value stocks. If all your growth managers jumped ship and started buying all value stocks, then your portfolio would have been 100% value stock at the end of 1993. You would have wound up with great performance but also you would have a lot of risk in your portfolio. So what is happening here is that your fund managers are putting you into a much higher risk profile without your agreeing to it or even knowing it."

Robin sighed. Roy looked down at the floor.

Asset Class Returns

Annual Returns for Key Indices (1982-2002) Ranked in order of performance (Best to Worst)

S&P 500 Index
Measures the performance of large capitalization U.S. Stocks. The S&P 500 is a market-value-weighted index of 500 stocks that are traded on the NYSE, AMEX and NASDAQ. The weightings make each company's influence on the Index performance directly proportional to that company's market value.

Russell 1000 Growth Index
Measures the performance of those Russell 1000 companies with higher price-to-book ratios and higher forecasted growth values.

Russell 1000 Value Index
Measures the performance of those Russell 1000 companies with lower price-to-book ratios and lower forecasted growth values.

MSCI Emerging Markets Free Index
A market-capitalization-weighted index made up of equities from 26 developing countries.

Russell 2000 Value Index
Contains those Russell 2000 securities with a below-average growth orientation. Securities in this index generally have lower price-to-book and price-to-earnings ratios than those in the Russell 2000 Growth Index.

Russell 2000 Growth Index
Contains those Russell 2000 securities with an above-average growth orientation. Securities in this index generally have higher price-to-book and price-to-earnings ratios than those in the Russell 2000 Value Index.

MSCI EAFE
A Morgan Stanley Capital International index that is designed to measure the performance of the developed stock markets of Europe, Australia, and the Far East.

LB Aggregate Bond
The Lehman Brothers Aggregate Bond index. This index includes U.S. government, corporate and mortgage-backed securities with maturities up to 30 years.

Salomon Brothers Non-U.S. Dollar World Government Bond Index
An index that includes institutionally traded bonds other than U.S. issues that have a fixed rate and a remaining maturity of 1 year or longer.

The MSCI Emerging Markets Global Index, Russell 1000 Value Index, and the Salomon Brothers Non - U.S. Dollar World Government Bond Index were not available prior to these dates.

The information presented is past performance. Past performance is no guarantee of future return. Investment return and principal value of a mutual fund investment will fluctuate so that an investor's shares on redemption may be worth more or less than the original cost.

In addition to the normal risks associated with equity investing, narrowly focused investments and investments in smaller companies typically exhibit higher volatility. International investments may involve risk of capital loss from unfavorable fluctuations in currency values, from differences in generally accepted accounting principles, or from economic or political instability in other nations.

The indices illustrated herein are unmanaged indices. You cannot invest in an index. Index returns do not reflect the impact of any management fees, transaction costs, or expenses. The index information seen here is for illustrative purposes only.

Mutual Fund Shares are not insured by the FDIC or any other agency, are not guaranteed by any financial institution, are not obligations of any financial institution, and involve investment risks, including possible loss of principal.

SEI Investments Management Corporation

Jay jumped in, "Look, there is a lot more to investment management than most people want to believe. When I got into the business in 1977, I thought the same as you—just pick some good low cost funds and you will be fine. Pretty soon I realized I was wrong. That's one reason why our firm went out and hired Brian as our Chief Investment Officer. Brian is a Chartered Financial Analyst (CFA). He's studied investments and the stock market his entire career. He was a great fit for us because our investment philosophy is to control risk while participating in the long-term performance of the market. Brian helped us put our philosophy into action." Jay turned to Brian. "Why don't you explain to Roy and Robin our approach and run through some recommendations for their portfolio."

"Sure," Brian said. "Remember we discussed your risk tolerance?"

"Yeah, some of the questions were hard to answer," Roy replied.

"No problem. You guys did fine," Brian said. "The results of that questionnaire tell us that given your ages, goals, and risk profile, you would be comfortable with an investment portfolio of 100% stocks. This is where most investors fall down. They never figure out the asset allocation part.

Robin nodded. "Okay. But tell us how this all works."

"We take the information from the risk tolerance discussion and put it into The Investment Portfolio Optimizer to determine the return you need to achieve all your goals that we discussed in The Progression of Wealth Blueprint," Jay replied. " When there is a disconnect between where you are comfortable investing and the return you need to meet your goals, some changes need to be made. The good news for you is we can achieve all your goals with an investment portfolio of 80% stocks and 20% fixed income. So we can actually reduce the risk level of your portfolio and still achieve all your goals."

"That sounds good to us", said Robin, looking encouragingly at Roy.

"It should," said Jay. "It's the best fit for you. We really like it when we can reduce our clients risk and meet their goals. It is much harder to do the reverse."

Roy looked pleased. "Great, go on."

"Once we have the asset allocation figured out, the rest is pretty simple," said Brian. "We develop an Investment Policy Statement (IPS) in writing that we will all agree to adhere to. Your IPS should include the following points." He showed them a sheet marked "Investment Policy Statement". *(See Appendix C for a copy of the Sewell's Investment Policy Statement.)*

- Your asset allocation
- Your time horizon
- The expected return
- The acceptable risk range of the portfolio
- Tax sensitivity
- The delineation of responsibilities
- Any other special considerations

"After the IPS is executed, the next step is to select the money managers to manage the portfolio," Brian continued. "The IPS is also something that needs to be given to the money managers to ensure that everyone is on the same page. Our money manager selection process includes a rigorous search and screening process to identify, evaluate, and select money managers that have a proven long-term track record in performance, risk management, and adherence to their investment process and discipline."

Jay took over. "Once these managers have been selected, they are constantly monitored. Every trade is monitored every day to ensure that there are no surprises. When a manager veers from its process or an integral member of their team leaves, a decision to keep the manager or replace the manager needs to be made. This kind of objectivity enables us to make informed decisions about our money managers to control the risk of the portfolio."

"There's a tax benefit, too," added Brian. "With constant monitoring of the managers for taxable portfolios we can control the tax aspects of that portfolio. For example, when we identify one manager incurring capital gains from their buying and selling decisions, we can request other managers to realize some losses in the portfolios to offset the capital gains. The result is a better after-tax performance than one can achieve through an indexing approach or through retail mutual funds."

"Is that why we had to pay so much in taxes last year?" Robin asked. "We didn't sell any of our mutual funds last year and we had to pay capital gains taxes. What was that all about?"

"Unfortunately, that is one of the major problems with retail mutual funds," Brian said. "Mutual funds by law are required to distribute at least once a year all the capital gains that they incurred during the year. But here is the problem. As the market ran up in the last few years most of the money managers were busy buying and selling stocks, which is known as portfolio turnover. Unfortunately, portfolio turnover means taxable transactions are occurring in your mutual funds. And by law the mutual funds must distribute these capital gains to their investors each year." He flipped the empty water bottle around in his hands. "It's a double-edged sword."

Brian got up and grabbed a round of spring water for the table. He came back and handed them out. "But we have discovered there are ways to control the capital gains taxes with certain portfolio techniques," Brian said. "However, most people are not aware of these techniques and the tax code is much too complicated for most people to effectively employ them. Again, while this is somewhat self-serving for us, investors need professional advisors to help them through the maze of complexity."

Roy looked up. "Damn straight. You know, I came into this meeting thinking differently, but you make a great case that we do need help. I don't have enough time to do it all, that's for sure."

"Most people don't," said Jay. "It is a full-time job. Believe me, we know."

Robin took a sip of water. "I'm in agreement on that, too," she said. "But once you get past that, how do we actually move our portfolio into the one you're recommending?"

"It's not so difficult," said Jay. "For starters, we have developed a tax-sensitive transition strategy to begin to reduce your concentration in your company stock. We can also reduce the tax consequences of selling some of your company stock by selling some of your mutual funds that have losses. We call this tax-loss pairing. We pair gains with losses so we have a zero tax cost."

"That's right," added Brian. "Once we implement your asset allocation strategy, we rebalance it on a quarterly basis."

"How does that work?" asked Robin.

"Your overall asset allocation is 80% stocks and 20% fixed income," answered Brian. "Below that we have multi-style asset classes such as large cap growth and large cap value and sub-styles beneath the asset classes. We will rebalance your portfolio every quarter back to the target weightings. So your portfolio will always be rebalanced back to 80% stock and 20% fixed income. And, until we change your asset allocation your portfolio will always be 80% stock and 20% fixed income. That's another way we control risk in your portfolio."

Roy looked perplexed. "I had always heard that you should cut your losses and let the winners run," he said. "What you described sounds different from that."

"What you just described is a Wall Street trader's mantra," said Jay. "We are not traders, or market timers—people who jump in and out of the market to grab market increases and avoid market decreases. This is an important difference. Let's face it, only traders on the floor of the exchanges have the access to information and the ability to implement trades quickly enough to profit from the information they have. Most investors do not have access to this level of information. So, investors really need to take a long-term approach to the stock market. The only proven way to effectively do this is 'time and diversification' and by controlling risk. That's what we do for you."

"Let me bring the point home in another example," said Brian. "Let's say you entered the market in 1988 and decided that you wanted 50% of your money in bonds and 50% in stocks. What do you think your portfolio would look like at the end of 1993 if you did nothing else?"

Roy shrugged. "I guess my stocks would have gone up a lot and the bonds would have gone up a little."

"Well, sort of," said Brian. "Actually, your stocks would have doubled and your bonds would have lost ground. Your portfolio would be about 70% stock and 30% bonds. But would that have been a good thing?" asked Brian"

"I'm not sure," said Robin. "I do know that we would have made money on the stocks."

"Yes, you would have," Brian answered. "Now, what will happen when stocks go down and bonds go up?"

Roy laughed. "I think I'm beginning to see the problem here."

"Right," Jay replied. "When you entered the market you decided that based on your goals and risks that you should have no more than 50% of your money in the stock market. Assuming nothing changed, allowing you to assume more risk, letting your allocation to get up to 70% stock is way too much risk for your portfolio. Had you rebalanced, you would have sold stocks as they went up and bought more bonds. You would be selling high and buying low. And your portfolio will be in exactly the right spot for when the stock market turns and the bond market moves ahead. It's the discipline of rebalancing that protects you. Left to their own decisions, investors have always done the opposite, they buy high and sell low. It's what Wall Street calls The Herd Mentality. If you go back in history, you will see money was pouring into stocks in the year following a great year and pouring into bonds after the stock market has a down year. Selling low and buying high. Add to that mix the psychology that investors refuse to sell their stocks when they go up because of tax ramifications and are afraid to sell stocks when they go down because of the hope that they will come back and you have a larger problem— decisions based on emotions tend to be wrong at the wrong time."

Robin nodded. "That's Roy, alright. He just hates to eat those losses."

Roy didn't argue. "That's me all over. But at some point don't you have to get out of the market altogether and wait it out like after 1987."

"No. Never," said Jay and Brian, nearly in unison. "No one over any extended period of time can effectively time the stock market," said Brian. "If you look at the movement of money over the past decade, investors have consistently done the wrong thing at the wrong time. Currently, this is happening with international stocks and emerging market companies. These asset classes have had good gains the past few years. People are pouring money into these asset classes and all are up double digits. Why? Because these stocks are hot right now—at least in the eyes of most investors—and these are the hot new asset classes. The problem is that these investors are always too late to these assets."

Jay pulled out another document among the papers on the table. "We performed a study of all the money managers we work with over the past 10 years and 15 years. All the money managers returned between 8 to 11% over the 10 and 15 year periods. A study released by DALBAR revealed that the individual investor in retail and discount brokerage accounts only returned 4–5% over the same 10 to 15 year periods[1]. That's half of what the professionals did. Why? Because the individuals played around with market timing too much and bought high and sold low. Market timing is like a bar of soap. The more you play with it, the less you have."

Roy and Robin appeared lost in thought.

Jay spoke up. "Look, if there was really a get rich quick scheme out there, why would all these professionals need to work? Wouldn't they just be sitting on their yachts enjoying their money? Why do they need to work everyday just like you? The stock market isn't where you get rich. That said, it will help you protect and grow your money. When you think of the market in these terms, it becomes clear that a disciplined long-term investment strategy that utilizes professional money managers, tremendous asset class diversification,

---

1. Ten-year period from 1990 to 2000, 15-year period from 1985 to 2000.

portfolio rebalancing, and tax-sensitivity is the only way you can participate in the rewards of the stock market and manage risk."

"Wow—I'm on board," said Roy. Robin nodded. "Me, too. Let's get our portfolio on the right track."

"Hey, we've already started to," said Brian.

Thirty minutes later, on the ride home, Roy shook his head. "You know I thought we had this covered. Boy, who was I kidding?"

"Well," Robin said, "you did the best you could. But you are busy at work. Think how much time you spend on your company and your people. Jay and Brian are saying that someone needs to spend the same amount of time managing our finances. I feel good that we have someone who will be keeping an eye on our investments full-time. It really gives me some peace of mind."

"Yeah, me too," added Roy. "I thought I would feel inadequate handing over our investments to someone else. But if I can redirect my focus and energy from worrying about our portfolio to my company and my career, I can make more money and probably work less doing it."

Robin laughed.

"What's so funny?" Roy asked.

"That's exactly what Jay and Brian said the Progression of Wealth would do—it's right for us because we need someone to take care of our finances from start to finish."

Roy laughed ruefully. "It is pretty funny when you think about it," he said. "Think about how many coaches and advisors we worked with to get ahead in our careers. Yet we felt we should go it alone in our personal financial lives."

"Right," said Robin. "And if we had treated our household as a business we would have been on the right track years ago." She sighed. "But at least we finally realized we need help. I feel good."

"Me, too," said Roy. In fact, I feel so good that I'm taking you to the Palm for dinner."

"You're the man," said Robin. "I'm starving."

April 5, 2003

Roy hung up the phone in the kitchen.

"Who was that on the phone, honey?" asked Robin. She was working on a client file at the dining room table with her laptop.

"It was Bob," answered Roy.

"How are he and Jane doing?" Robin wanted to know.

"Not so great," said Roy with a sigh. "Our company just asked him to leave—he's being downsized."

"Oh no!" said Robin. "I wonder what happened. What are he and Jane going to do? Can he retire?"

"No," said Roy, "that's what he called about."

"He started working there before you did, didn't he?" asked Robin.

"Yeah, and he's 60 years old," said Roy. He's panicking because he lost most of his retirement money in the stock market over the past three years and doesn't think he can retire."

"Why did he call you?" asked Robin.

"He wanted my advice," said Roy, taking a seat at the table across from Robin. "He said he sees how happy we are and the life we live and he wanted to know where he went wrong."

"What did you tell him?"

"I gave him Jay and Brian's number and recommended he call them. I told him having someone to help with his finances, especially at a time like this, would be invaluable," said Roy, toying with a pen.

"I'm just glad we got to Jay and Brian over ten years ago or we would be in the same boat as Bob and Jane," sighed Robin. "It's really a shame. They're such nice people."

"It really is a shame," said Roy. "What's even a bigger shame is that there are a lot of people in Bob's situation. They were way too aggressive with their investments and took a beating over the past 3 years. Now retirement isn't an option for them." Roy shook his head.

Roy paused and thought about how his investment philosophy had taken shape over the past 10 years. How had he and Robin been so lucky when so many people suffered such huge losses in the stock market? "TIME AND DIVERSIFICATION, of course," mused Roy. Jay and Brian must have said that phrase to him hundreds of times over the past ten years. But it was true. "Time and diversification allowed them to meet their goals.

"We're just lucky we got the "TIME AND DIVERSIFICATION" mantra into our daily vocabulary," he said finally.

"That's great, honey. Jay and Brian must be very proud of their protégé," laughed Robin. "Remember when you called them up in 1998 and asked Brian to move our portfolio into technology stocks? What was the term you used?" She paused, looking up at the ceiling. "Oh! Now I remember.

'Juice up our investments.' How could I forget? That one was a keeper." She chuckled.

"Yeah, I remember, and then I got an hour-long lecture from Jay and Brian about the long-term returns of the stock market and how all I needed was time and diversification," grinned Roy. "No instant juicing going on there."

"Yeah, but you wore them down and they agreed to let you open a discount brokerage account to trade stocks and options," said Robin. "It seemed like a fair compromise."

"It did indeed," agreed Roy. "At the time."

"But what is that account worth today?" asked Robin with a small smirk.

"About $25,000 in tax losses," joked Roy. "It was worth over $100,000 at one point. I think Brian used the losses to offset the capital gains on my company stock options. I hate when they're right," grinned Roy.

"I remember another good one, Roy," Robin continued, leaning back in her chair. "Remember a year later when they recommended we start moving more of our stock portfolio into bonds?"

"Yeah, I thought they were nuts, especially with the market nearly 40% that year," said Roy. "I still remember their rationale. Jay said we were about three to four years from retirement and it was time to take some of the risk out of the portfolio as we geared up for retirement. Another great move by Jay and Brian, another instance where I had to admit that they were right," said Roy.

"They always said they never try to time the market. They simply said as long as they get our time horizon right and our stomach for risk, we would be fine," said Robin, typing something onto her laptop.

"They were right," said Roy. "Think about everything we lived through the past 10 years." He started listing them on his fingers. "The widespread use of the Internet by the public. The dot com explosion. Irrational exuberance. Then the dot com implosion. The Enron scandal and 9/11. Not to mention the massive corporate scandals and fraud. And the fall of Arthur Anderson." He sat back and emitted a low whistle. "All that leading to an unparalleled three-year bear market the likes of which has never been seen before. We've survived a lot. And we came out relatively unscathed." He smiled.

"All because of that mantra—TIME AND DIVERSIFICATION," said Robin, her fingers still clicking on the keys. "And quarterly rebalancing. A systematic way to buy low and sell high."

"Anyone's dream come true," sighed Roy. "And through all this, the long-term performance of the stock market is still between 10 to 12%. This was one of the best things Jay and Brian taught us. Who would have thought one of the Marx Brothers came up with the asset allocation stuff?" mused Roy.

"It was Markowicz and it was called the Modern Portfolio Theory," Robin corrected Roy. "You know—the idea that over 90% of investment success is how you allocate your assets."

"Markowicz, Malkoviwz, Marx, whatever. Whoever he was, he was a good man and I'm glad Jay and Brian knew about him," laughed Roy. "That concept and the fact that Jay and Brian met with us quarterly to update us on our plan and the stock market kept us from worrying about our investments unnecessarily."

"Thank God for that. One less thing to worry about," said Robin. She gave a final click on her laptop, looking satisfied, and turned it off. "I hope they can help Bob and Jane," said Robin. "I hope it's not too late."

"Don't worry honey, I'm sure Jay and Brian will get them back on track," said Roy trying to comfort Robin.

"If they can't, no one can," said Robin closing her laptop.

Chapter 4 Overview:
The Investment Portfolio Optimizer™

The Investment Portfolio Optimizer evaluates your investment portfolio to determine whether your asset allocation is appropriate for the return needed to meet your goals. In addition, the risk inherent in your portfolio is evaluated and compared to your Risk Profile to ensure you are comfortable with the amount of risk being taken. The goal of The Investment Portfolio Optimizer is to optimize the return needed for you to meet your goals while taking the least amount of risk. You should have an asset allocation specifically tailored to you and your goals.

Chapter 5

THE CASH FLOW OPTIMIZER

"Talk about your plenty, talk about your ills,
one man gathers what another man spills."
— Jerry Garcia / Robert Hunter

April 30, 2000

ROY SEWELL WOKE UP on a warm, spring Saturday morning feeling better than he had in years.

He opened his bedroom window to let some fresh air inside and felt the first reassuring balms of spring drift into the bedroom. Birds were singing, the sun was shining, and some of the boys down the block had already begun playing baseball—he could hear them shouting and laughing. Roy thought to himself, all these years living in this house and I never noticed that sound before. Then he realized what was missing: the kids. This was the first spring that both Jack and Morgan were away in college. He'd thought the days when the kids weren't home anymore was so far off, but here they were. Just he and Robin. The house was quiet, allowing him to hear the sounds outside, and he reminisced about all the baseball and softball games he and Robin had gone to for Jack and Morgan. It made him feel good inside.

Funny thing about baseball, he thought. Here, all the talk between he and Robin all those years—and with Jay and Brian, too—had been about making plans, meeting goals and executing a solid financial plan. And that was fine—in fact, he'd really enjoyed working on his family's own Progression of Wealth program and relished how well things had worked out financially.

That—and the fact that his family was happy and healthy—was a big reason for how good he'd been feeling of late.

But it wasn't just about feeling good. He felt confident, too. Confident that his family's future was bright and confident in his own ability to continue making his mark in the bio-technology world and making his clients—as well as his family—happy, too.

Something struck him while watching an old show on ESPN Classic television the night before. It was a profile on baseball legend Pete Rose. In one segment, the reporters were talking to Rose while he took batting practice. One questioner, noting that Rose needed 97 hits to pass Hall-of-Famer Ty Cobb as the all-time baseball hitting champion, asked Rose how many at bats would it take to get the 97 hits he needed.

"97," Rose answered, slapping another line drive into the outfield.

"97?" replied the shocked reporter. "Why, that means a 1,000 batting average —97 hits in 97 at-bats. Nobody could do that."

Rose stopped hitting and wiped the sweat off his forehead. "Look, I'm in the confidence business," he said to the reporter. "I go up to the plate each time confident I'm going to get a hit. No exceptions."

It was a lesson in confidence that made a deep impression on Roy Sewell. Sales was a confidence business, too. Maybe the ultimate confidence business. And financial planning was a confidence business, too. You had to develop a good blueprint and have the *cojones* to execute it and allow it to work. He'd lost sight of that before he and Robin had met with Jay and Brian and started working on the Progression of Wealth. In the process, he had lost confidence in himself as well. Ten years ago, he wasn't sure that he could secure a financial future for his family.

He recalled Rose ending the interview by saying that as long as he was prepared and had a plan there was no reason why he shouldn't get a base hit every time he stepped into the batter's box. Why shouldn't it be the same for Roy? Take his sales career. Sure, he knew that he couldn't make every sale. But he could believe he could get every customer of his to sign on the bottom line—but only if he believed in himself. After all, there was no point in meeting a client if he thought it wouldn't result in a sale at some point. That would be negative thinking and negative thinkers don't last long in the sales game. Now he was responsible to teach his ten sales managers and 50 salespeople the same lessons he had to learn.

He padded into the bathroom to wash up, feeling calmer about things. Splashing some cold water on his face, he felt like something inside of him had changed over the past ten years. The talks he had had with Jay and Brian about the Progression of Wealth—and the way their plan had performed so successfully—had changed the way he'd looked at his career and himself. Roy Sewell had begun to see things a bit more clearly—the Rose interview was a good example of that—and he began feeling that he was ready to tackle the world once again after those uncertain years when he couldn't make a sale to save his life, let alone secure a financial future for his family. If nothing else, that was a change for the better.

He got dressed and walked downstairs. Looking out the French doors into the back yard, he saw Robin working on her garden. Robin's new garden was already planted—he'd done the digging himself—and that always brightened her mood. Robin had taken some of the packages of seed he'd bought at Stateline Garden & Supply and planted them, careful to choose a good patch of land in the yard, careful to space things out and look out for the sunny and the shady areas, just like she always had. It hadn't rained in a few days so she was watering, lazily letting the cold water arch over the few feet of stone steps and grass leading to the garden and onto her plants. She looked content, too.

Robin always liked the early spring season—the return to warm-season flower and vegetable growing. She liked how the blooming of her dogwoods and azaleas coincided, without fail, with the return of the robins and the hummingbirds that flitted about her garden. "It's daylight savings time," she thought to herself. "More daylight and more time in my garden." While she was watering she noticed that some of the leaves on her tomato and pepper plants were a little frayed. "Damn!" she thought. "Bugs."

She also noticed that some weeds had cropped up between her plants. Sighing, she bent down to pull them up, making a mental note to grab some Weed-Be-Gon® at the garden store later on that day.

She finished up her watering, taking particular care with the Easter Lilies she'd bought a few weeks back. She'd planted the sturdy flowers with their strong stems with some ginger to add to their greenery. In a few weeks, they'd be in full bloom—if the bugs and weeds didn't get them first.

Twenty minutes later, after putting her garden tools away and rolling the garden hose up, Robin was back in the kitchen with Roy, who had brewed some

Dark Peruvian Blend coffee and laid out a tray of fresh egg bagels with some honey-flavored cream cheese. "What to do today, Hon, what to do," she said.

"Oh, I don't know," Roy said. "Go down to the bank, jump into the vault, and roll around in all our money like Scrooge McDuck?"

"You're a scream," she said, patting his back affectionately. "A real laugh riot." She took a bagel and spread some cream cheese on it. She decided to change the subject. "Is it me or are things going real well, lately?"

Roy nodded. "I was thinking the same thing myself. It really seems like we're operating on all cylinders. I mean, we've just about met all our goals, especially the ones we laid out in our progression of wealth blueprint."

"Yeah, I noticed that, too," said Robin. "Do you remember when Jay and Brian first told us about the importance of setting goals—that you couldn't meet your financial goals if you didn't have any?"

"The guys were talking about the Cash Flow something or other," Roy replied.

"The Cash Flow Optimizer, Einstein."

"Yeah, that's it," said Roy snapping his fingers. "That was the first time in our life we ever made a budget. I couldn't believe how much we were spending compared to our peers."

June 21, 1994 (six years earlier)

Jay opened the meeting with a question. "Ever heard the phrase 'Cash is King'? Well, for our purposes let's say 'Cash Flow is King'. In its purest form, cash flow is simply the difference, or net, of the inflows and the outflows—income less expenses."

Jay and Brian had met with the Sewells at a local restaurant and bar, and were seated on the outside deck enjoying some cocktails and the late afternoon summer breeze.

"We have worked with hundreds of business owners since 1977," Jay continued, sipping from his drink. "Every successful business owner has the same thing in common. They know their cash flow down to the last dollar. This is worth repeating—successful business owners know their cash flow down to the last dollar. The businesses are very different and their management style also very different, but these owners know exactly when and where the next dollar is coming from and how to keep those dollars."

"So how does this apply to us?" asked Roy, fiddling with a cocktail napkin.

"It's leading to my explanation of something that will help you, something we call The Cash Flow Optimizer. The Cash Flow Optimizer is a unique tool that helps you determine how much money you have to invest to reach your financial goals," Jay explained. "It also serves as a budgeting tool if you're not saving enough. As you move on into stages two and three of The Cash Flow Optimizer, it also serves as a tool to help you give away wealth if you have exceeded your financial goals and wish to help others, such as charity or your family. The beauty of the Optimizer is that it is a multi-purpose tool to help you accomplish savings, budgeting, and gifting. It's really multi-functional, like a baseball player who can hit, field, run, and throw."

"So cash flow optimization uses the techniques that successful business owners have been employing," Brian picked up. "The first step is to identify all your sources of income. We recommend using recurring predictable income. Recurring and predictable income is income that is very probable of being received in the future. For example, if you have a base salary and a bonus structure, but the bonus may or may not be received each year, then don't include it in your income. Another example is capital gains. Just because you had large capital gain distributions one year doesn't mean you will have them again in future years. For income, err on the side on conservatism. Go lighter rather than heavier. I have a list of examples of income items," said Brian, taking out some sheets from his briefcase. "Most of the income items listed below can be taken from your income tax return." Roy and Robin leaned in to look at the list.

SOURCES OF INCOME:

Salary and Wages

Bonus

Partnership Distributions

Business Income

Dividends and Income

Rental Income

Total Income

"Now for the harder part," said Jay. "Your expenses. Again, take a lesson from the business owner. The business owner knows the expenses just as well as the income. Itemizing your expenses is generally a time-consuming exercise. But the investment of time is well worth it."

"We took the information from the Budget Worksheet that you completed and put the information into The Cash Flow Optimizer. Ready to discuss the results?" asked Brian.

"That depends," said Robin. "Are they good results, or did we flunk out a lot like on our report card?"

Jay smiled. "This is a little different. No grades on this one." Robin looked relieved and sipped her white wine.

"It's fairly basic," Brian said, taking a drink from his glass of water before continuing. "The Cash Flow Optimizer is divided into three stages. Stage One is the savings years of your life, which should begin the day you graduate college." He placed his drink down on the table and took a pen out of his pocket. He grabbed a notepad from his briefcase and started drawing a diagram. "It could, however, begin when you are 30 years old or anywhere between 30 to 50 years old." He drew three vertical columns down the length of the paper. "This is the stage when you are saving for your children's college, you're beginning a strong retirement savings plan, and also accomplishing many other goals during this stage, like purchasing your first or perhaps even a second home. Typically this is a time where it is very difficult to save because of all the expenses of raising a family."

"You got the expensive part right," said Roy. A waitress appeared with a large bowl of shrimp and cocktail sauce, and Roy dove in. "Don't mind the munching," he said. "I'm still listening."

"Stage Two begins the heavy savings part of your life—what we call pre-retirement," Brian said, writing the word "pre-retirement" at the top of the second column. "This is at a time, normally between 45 and 55 years old, where your children have finished college, they have left the house and are beginning their careers. It is a time that you and your spouse have for yourself and also a time where your expenses may be reduced, and gives you the ability to start saving tremendously for the next stage, which may be retirement or financial independence."

"This part I'm liking," said Roy. "Especially the part about the kids moving out of the house." He grinned.

"Stage Three is the retirement years," Brian continued, writing the term on top of the third column. "This is the time of your life where you no longer are potentially saving money, but you are actually drawing money out and spending it, and this can be spending it on yourself, on your family, gifting to charity, things of that nature."

He stopped and slid the paper over to the Sewells, who studied it closely.

"We think that the Optimizer, if done at an early age, can help you identify when you'll be able to reach financial independence," Jay said. "Many people like to save enough in Stage One that, by the time they hit Stage Two they may still be working, but savings are not a major goal. They would rather spend the money that they did not spend in Stage One. Typically, these are very fortunate people who have really concentrated very diligently in Stage One."

Roy cleared his throat. "You mean people like us?"

"Right," Jay replied. "But for those who have not done so, then Stage Two is the time to really start that type of savings program.

"As you can see on this page we have worksheets for your Stage One" he said, producing some pages. "The first column is your current spending in each of these categories. The second is the percent of your income. The third is the benchmark column, which is taken as a percent of your income under the percentage benchmarks. Once again, the benchmarks should only be used as a guide." He looked at the Sewells to make sure they understood. "Typically, we feel at Stage One at least 15 to 20% of your earnings should go towards savings. This is of your gross earnings, not your net earnings. You'll see the benchmark under Stage One shows you how this is accomplished in that stage. Remember, this is only a benchmark and if you can save more, the better off you'll be in Stage Two and Stage Three."

Robin and Roy looked on attentively, nodding every now and then.

"One thing to keep in mind is that when you get to Stage Three there is no real need for savings and money will be spent at some level," Jay said. "If your philosophy is to continue to save, and you're pulling money out of your retirement accounts and then putting it back in to save, that's your prerogative. We think that Stage Three should be a time when you are enjoying life, spending money, and doing the things that you really want to accomplish." He shrugged his shoulders. "But, if you can accomplish this in Stage Two, more power to you."

Robin shook her head. "Not in our current situation. No sir."

Jay nodded. "Okay, that's fine." He turned back to the workbook. "On Stage One, you'll be able to see that the benchmarks for each category indicate that you should spend approximately 19% to 20% in liability expenses.

You should spend no more then 8% to 9% for recreational expenses and 5% for insurance. Other household expenses should be approximately 18% to 20% and miscellaneous expenses should be approximately 2% per year."

The Cash Flow Optimizer™

Client Name	**Roy and Robin Sewell**
Stage	**Stage 1**
Current Income	**200,000**

			Stage 1		
	Current Spending	% of Income	Benchmark $	Benchmark %	Variance $
LIABILITIES					
Mortgage Payment (P&I).........	$33,251	16.63%	32,000	16.00%	($1,251)
Real Estate Taxes.............	$6,800	3.40%	6,667	3.33%	($133)
Second Home Mortgage.........		0.00%	-	0.00%	$0
Real Estae Taxes..............		0.00%	-	0.00%	$0
Rent or Lease Payments........		0.00%	-	0.00%	$0
Equity Loans........................		0.00%	-	0.00%	$0
Automobile Loans.................		0.00%	-	0.00%	$0
Personal Loans....................		0.00%	-	0.00%	$0
Credit Cards........................		0.00%	-	0.00%	$0
Store Charge Accounts..........		0.00%	-	0.00%	$0
Other:_____ 0		0.00%	-	0.00%	$0
TOTAL.............................	**$40,051**	**20.03%**	**38,667**	**19.33%**	**($1,384)**
INCOME & SOCIAL SECURITY TAXES					
Client Federal......................	$15,000	7.50%	14,740	7.37%	($260)
Spouse Federal....................	$15,000	7.50%	14,740	7.37%	($260)
Client State.........................	$2,800	1.40%	2,800	1.40%	$0
Spouse State.......................	$2,800	1.40%	2,800	1.40%	$0
Client Local.........................	$135	0.07%	140	0.07%	$5
Spouse Local.......................	$135	0.07%	140	0.07%	$5
Client Social Security.............	$5,320	2.66%	5,320	2.66%	$0
Spouse Social Security..........	$5,320	2.66%	5,320	2.66%	$0
Other:_____		0.00%	.	0.00%	$0
TOTAL.............................	**$46,510**	**23.26%**	**46,000**	**23.00%**	**($510)**
TRANSPORTATION					
Auto Leases........................	$8,300	4.15%	12,000	6.00%	$3,700
Gas & Oil............................	$2,500	1.25%	2,773	1.39%	$273
Maintenance & Repair..........	$1,200	0.60%	1,333	0.67%	$133
License & Registration..........	$135	0.07%	133	0.07%	($2)
Public Transportation.............		0.00%	-	0.00%	$0
Parking & Tolls....................	$350	0.18%	400	0.20%	$50
Road Use/Excise Taxes.........		0.00%	-	0.00%	$0
Other:_____		0.00%	-	0.00%	$0
TOTAL.............................	**$12,485**	**6.24%**	**16,640**	**8.32%**	**$4,155**

The Cash Flow Optimizer™

Client Name	**Roy and Robin Sewell**
Stage	**Stage 1**
Current Income	**200,000**

	Current Spending	% of Income	Benchmark $	Benchmark %	Variance $
INSURANCE					
Life Insurance......................	$560	0.28%	1,200	0.60%	$640
Disability Insurance...............	$886	0.44%	1,333	0.67%	$447
Medical Insurance..................	$0	0.00%	800	0.40%	$800
Automobile Insurance.............	$2,700	1.35%	2,667	1.33%	($33)
Home Owner's Insurance.........	$900	0.45%	800	0.40%	($100)
Flood Insurance.....................		0.00%	-	0.00%	$0
Earthquake Insurance.............		0.00%	-	0.00%	$0
Other:_____		0.00%	-	0.00%	$0
TOTAL...............................	**$5,046**	**2.52%**	**6,800**	**3.40%**	**$1,754**
RECREATION					
Dining Out............................	$7,200	3.60%	6,933	3.47%	($267)
Movies................................	$1,500	0.75%	1,387	0.69%	($113)
Concerts..............................		0.00%	-	0.00%	$0
Vacations.............................	$3,500	1.75%	4,000	2.00%	$500
Hobbies...............................	$2,100	1.05%	1,333	0.67%	($767)
Entertaining..........................	$1,200	0.60%	800	0.40%	($400)
Country Club.........................		0.00%	-	0.00%	$0
Summer Camp......................		0.00%	-	0.00%	$0
Sporting Events....................		0.00%	-	0.00%	$0
Theater and Opera................	$250	0.13%	400	0.20%	$150
Other:_____	$0	0.00%	-	0.00%	$0
TOTAL...............................	**$15,750**	**7.88%**	**14,853**	**7.43%**	**($897)**
HOUSEHOLD EXPENSES					
Groceries.............................	$15,000	7.50%	13,867	6.93%	($1,133)
Condo & Association Fees.....	$0	0.00%	-	0.00%	$0
Clothing...............................	$3,200	1.60%	2,133	1.07%	($1,067)
Electricity.............................	$2,400	1.20%	2,400	1.20%	$0
Gas....................................	$2,100	1.05%	2,400	1.20%	$300
Telephone............................	$1,000	0.50%	960	0.48%	($40)
Cable TV..............................	$580	0.29%	560	0.28%	($20)
Water & Sewage...................	$920	0.46%	960	0.48%	$40
Waste Disposal....................		0.00%	-	0.00%	$0
Child Care...........................		0.00%	7,700	3.85%	$7,700
Lawn Care...........................	$800	0.40%	800	0.40%	$0
Household Maintenance.........	$4,200	2.10%	2,671	1.34%	($1,529)
Other:_____		0.00%	-	0.00%	$0
TOTAL...............................	**$30,200**	**15.10%**	**34,451**	**17.23%**	**$4,251**

The Cash Flow Optimizer™

Client Name	**Roy and Robin Sewell**
Stage	**Stage 1**
Current Income	**200,000**

	Stage 1				
	Current Spending	% of Income	Benchmark $	Benchmark %	Variance $
MISCELLANEOUS					
Barber/Hair Salon..................	$400	0.20%	320	0.16%	($80)
Professional Dues................		0.00%	-	0.00%	$0
Newspapers & Subscriptions...	$250	0.13%	333	0.17%	$83
Medical & Dental...................	$1,400	0.70%	1,067	0.53%	($333)
Pet Care............................		0.00%	-	0.00%	$0
Domestic Help.....................	$0	0.00%	1,120	0.56%	$1,120
Children's Allowances............	$3,500	1.75%	2,000	1.00%	($1,500)
Lessons.............................	$1,200	0.60%	-	0.00%	($1,200)
Education/Schooling.............	$5,500	2.75%	-	0.00%	($5,500)
Cosmetics/Personal Care.......	$550	0.28%	733	0.37%	$183
Dry Cleaning.......................	$420	0.21%	400	0.20%	($20)
Other:_____		0.00%	-	0.00%	$0
TOTAL.............................	$13,220	6.61%	5,973	2.99%	($7,247)
GIFTS					
Birthdays...........................	$300	0.15%	267	0.13%	($33)
Anniversaries......................	$250	0.13%	267	0.13%	$17
Weddings...........................	$200	0.10%	400	0.20%	$200
Showers............................		0.00%	-	0.00%	$0
Christmas..........................	$800	0.40%	667	0.33%	($133)
Hanukkah...........................		0.00%	-	0.00%	$0
Bar/Bat Mitzvahs..................		0.00%	-	0.00%	$0
Charity	$400	0.20%	667	0.33%	$267
Other:_____		0.00%	-	0.00%	$0
TOTAL.............................	$1,950	0.98%	2,267	1.13%	$317
Totals	$165,212	82.61%	$165,651	82.83%	$439
Available for Savings	34,788		34,349		$439

SAVINGS & INVESTMENTS					
401k- Client	$10,000	5.00%	10,000	5.00%	$0
401k- spouse		0.00%	-	0.00%	$0
Ira's	$2,000	1.00%	2,000	1.00%	$0
Savings Account...................		0.00%	10,349	5.17%	$10,349
College Savings Plans		0.00%	12,000	6.00%	$12,000
Other:_____		0.00%	-	0.00%	$0
TOTAL.............................	$12,000	6.00%	34,349	17.17%	$22,349
Excess	$22,788		-	100.00%	

"What about gifts?" Robin asked. "We both come from big families."

Jay looked down at the workbook. "Gifts, which are typically a personal decision, especially in the area of charity, should be 1% to 2% if you guys are going to accomplish your savings goals. But if you choose to give more away to charity then this possibly will reduce your overall savings goals, so just be aware of this."

"Where do you get all these statistics?" Roy asked, reaching for another shrimp.

"From a proprietary financial planning database that contains data for families in the same demographic and income class as you. The database is cross-checked against the government's statistics ," Brian said. "We feel that we're really locked in on these percentages."

"Take your situation, for example," Jay said, taking a shrimp. "You guys are in Stage One, with a current income of $200,000. And, based on the budget you prepared you have a current spending level of $177,212. If we subtract the $177,212 from your income you should have available $22,788 for savings. The benchmark savings for you is $34,349." He sipped his drink, then took out his calculator and started punching in some numbers. "If you go on to The Cash Flow Optimizer you'll notice that you included your savings of $12,000 to your retirement plans. If we add this to the $22,788 you have the ability to save $34,788." He punched in some more numbers. "Let's see—that's about $540 over the benchmark savings." He closed the calculator and popped it back into his coat pocket.

Brian spoke. "As you can see from the Stage One analysis, you currently have the ability to save a good amount. And when we look at your financial independence expander, which comes a bit later, we'll look at additional opportunities to save more which will further allow you to meet your financial goals."

"So, after a careful review, we see that in essence your savings ability is well within the benchmark," Jay added. "That's how it works." What you haven't done, however, is identify a way to ensure that you save that $34,788 each and every year that you can. This is where the real power of the Cash Flow Optimizer comes in. It shows you how to save the money. Below is the Action Plan that we developed for you." He turned the paper around so the Sewells could see.

1) Continue to maximize Roy's 401(k) account for annual savings of $10,000. *(See Sidebar.)*

2) Begin to save $1,000 per month to UGMA accounts for your kids' education. *(See Sidebar.)*

3) Begin to save $900 per month to a taxable account.

4) At the end of each year fund a retirement plan for Robin.

The 2001 Tax Law expanded the amount that individuals can contribute to company-sponsored retirement accounts such as 401(k) accounts: (Note: the 2003 tax law did not change any of the amounts.)

- *$12,000 in 2003*
- *$13,000 in 2004*
- *$14,000 in 2005*
- *$15,000 in 2006*

In addition, a special catch-up provision was enacted for employees over 50 years old allowing additional contributions:

- *$2,000 in 2003*
- *$3,000 in 2004*
- *$4,000 in 2005*
- *$5,000 in 2006*

The 2001 Tax Law also allows you to save for college education tax-free through the amendments to college savings plans or Section 529 Plans. Anyone saving for college should consider how a 529 Plan fits into their educational savings plan. Some of the key highlights of the 529 Plans are:

- *Tax-Free Savings*
- *No Income Limits*
- *High Contribution Limits*
- *Adult Owner Controls Account*
- *Ability to Change Beneficiary*
- *Contributions are a Completed Gift*

"We recommend saving on a monthly systematic basis directly from your checking account. It works just like your 401(k) savings. You pay yourself first each and every month," said Jay.

Robin interrupted. "But what we currently like is that the money in our checking account is available in case of emergencies and for home projects, vacations, and the like."

"We hear this objection all the time," answered Brian. "We know that once the money gets into your checking account there is little chance that it will get saved. It will disappear. As much as you resist it, it will get spent," Brian assured them.

"You are right," said Roy. "We always find a way to spend it. Or the kids do, anyway, asking for advances on their allowance."

Robin chimed in. "But where do we get money from when we need it? I don't want to strap ourselves each month just to meet our savings goal."

"That's where the Financial Independence Cultivator comes in. It develops a strategy to allow you to meet your short-term goals. It already showed you the cash reserves you should have on hand, and what to save and how to save to meet those short-term goals. And at the end of the day your investments are always available if and when you need them," said Jay.

"That makes sense, I guess," said Robin, crunching an ice cube from her glass.

"It really works," said Jay. "Let The Progression of Wealth Process show you the way."

Later that night, Robin poured two glasses of iced tea and brought them out to the patio. Roy was sprawled out on a deck chair reading *Business Week*.

"Look at this," he said. "A recent survey by a large consulting firm shows that unless we save a great deal more than we currently do, three out of four Americans over the age of 20 will have less than half the money they need to retire and maintain their pre-retirement standard of living."

"Jeez," Robin said, placing the glasses of tea on the glass patio table, being careful to slide coasters underneath. "Three out of four?"

"Three out of four," Roy said. "In fact, on average they would have to reduce their expenses by 60%—or get a job flipping burgers—in order to make it through their twilight years without running out of money."

He flipped the page.

"Wait, there's more. If your after-tax expenses currently run $50,000 a year and you retire today, you would have to cut your spending by at least

$30,000 if you want your money to last as long as you do. And that huge cut in your budget assumes that you have the good sense to die on the day you spend your last penny. If you survive longer than the actuaries estimate, you'll outlive your money."

Robin sat down and exhaled. "Well, that's why setting long-term financial goals is so critical. Fortunately, Jay says it's pretty easy." She took a drink and thought. "And we really do have the ability to save more, we both know we do."

"We really do need to get serious about our savings strategy. Let's give it a try," said Roy. "Or we could always just go back to our old way of doing things haphazardly."

Setting Financial Goals

Here are some ideas that will help you establish your goal-setting game plan:

- *Be specific — Aim for clear targets such as "$2,000 into a retirement account," rather than generalities like "contribute to savings."*

- *Put pay raises directly into savings or toward debt reduction — If you make ends meet now, then you don't need to live off the cash you get in a pay raise. That being the case, put the extra money where it will do the most good, either increasing retirement savings or trimming debt. In this way, you maximize the good of the pay raise and move toward long-term goals without reducing your standard of living.*

- *Invest in equities — It is virtually impossible to beat inflation and generate a decent return without investing in the stock market. You're taking on investment risk, but you are avoiding inflation risk, and if you have a diversified portfolio, you are spreading your investment risk. Inflation risk isn't to be understated, even though it's been relatively non-existent for the past several years. Let's say you're heavily invested in Treasuries that pay 6% interest. Inflation suddenly spikes upward to 10%. You're now losing money and the only way to compensate is to sell those investments at a loss and reinvest the money or to continue falling further behind in real income because inflation is outstripping the return on your investments.*

- *Estimate how much you'll need to retire in comfort* — Start with a rough estimate based on what you earn now. If you expect a more modest life in retirement, use 60% to 70% of your current income. However, if the future holds too many unknowns, start with 100%. Then tackle more detailed financial calculations—either on your own or with the help of financial planners-to assess such factors as the likely impact inflation will have on your purchasing power.

- *Develop a savings plan* — How far away you are from retirement plays a large part in how you should invest your retirement money. Historically, there are three stages to a long-term regular savings plan for retirement: capitalization, consolidation, and conservation. In the first stage, people should be most concerned with building up their retirement savings portfolio. These investors can take as aggressive an outlook as their nerves can stand because at this point there is little capital to risk. The second step, consolidation, makes up the bulk of your savings plan; balance the aggressive investments with some tamer ones, to better protect your existing assets. The final change, from consolidation to conservation, when your investments should aim to preserve the capital you have, should take place one to three years before you retire. The exact timing of all these should take current market conditions into account.

- *Start saving now* — You'll need to save enough from your 30-odd years of working to live for 20+ years in retirement. So get cracking. When you do ramp up your savings program, overestimate your needs. It's far better to end up with too much money than not enough. Even a little bit more a year can make a difference in the long term.

- *Get some good life insurance* — Solid life insurance is critical to your family's fiscal fitness. Term is generally the most inexpensive way to insure a life. Term policies, however, offer no savings feature, build no cash value, or other tax-deferral opportunities. If the policyholder dies during the coverage period, the company pays a specified sum of money to the beneficiary. The key for deciding how much insurance to purchase is for each partner to determine how much money he or she would need to live comfortably.

"Yeah," said Robin, "haphazardly and half-assed. That's been the Sewell motto for way too long. I definitely think it's time for a change."

"I hope this works," Roy said, taking a drink from his glass. "I don't want to spend my Golden Years flipping burgers under the Golden Arches."

Chapter 5 Overview:
Cash Flow Optimizer™

The Cash Flow Optimizer will show you how to unlock your savings power. The Cash Flow Optimizer is a both a diagnostic and budgeting tool. You will learn how to identify opportunities to save more, or spend (gift) more, if appropriate. In addition, The Cash Flow Optimizer will allow you to project future cash flows to determine its effects on your Progression of Wealth.

Chapter 6

THE FINANCIAL INDEPENDENCE EXPANDER

*"All lies and jest; still a man hears what he wants to hear
and disregards the rest."*

– Paul Simon

September 10, 1999

"I HOPE JACK REMEMBERS to get me a diet soda and not regular," Roy said to Robin.

Robin did not look up from the program she was reading. "I'm sure he'll get it right," she said, turning the page. "He is in college, after all. Oh look, honey, here she is!"

Roy leaned over and looked at the spot on the page where Robin was pointing. He read aloud, "Morgan Sewell, flute soloist."

"Doesn't that have a nice ring to it?" asked Robin, setting the program down in her lap. "It's great to know that she's come this far since she started playing."

"She better have, for all the money I've spent on that instrument and those lessons!" joked Roy.

"Well, we're lucky that she was able to continue with that in high school," said Robin, taking her purse out from under the seat and rooting through it. "Not every school around here has such a good music program."

"Well, private schools do tend to have great music programs," said Roy. "I'm just glad she's so serious about continuing to play. That's our dollars at work!"

Robin finally found the tube of lip-gloss she was looking for and applied it. "Not to mention she's such a smart student. She's been on honor roll since she started here three years ago. Following in her big brother's footsteps!"

"Yeah, Jack's doing great," agreed Roy. "And he got to play on one of the best high school baseball teams in the state before going to college."

"And you know that the fact that he went to such a good high school gave him a big advantage for getting into college," said Robin. "Not only did his grades improve when he got here, but the school name certainly counts for something."

"And now think. He's at Villanova," said Roy proudly.

"Who would have thought we could afford Villanova?" Robin countered.

"Exactly. Before we started on The Progression of Wealth, we never would have imagined being able to afford a school like Villanova," said Roy, stretching in his seat. "But then again, only the best for my kids."

"Remember how we used to think that we'd have to tap into our retirement to be able to afford the kids' schooling?" asked Robin, picking up her program again. "It's a good thing we didn't count on that baseball scholarship you were sure of."

"Hey, he didn't get the scholarship but his skills certainly helped him get into 'Nova," said Roy. "He was definitely borderline with the grades and SAT scores but coming from a great private high school and being good at sports sure did help," said Roy.

"Very true," agreed Robin.

"Well, I'm just glad we are able to afford it," said Roy. He leaned over to look at the program with Robin. "That looks really nice, honey." He and Robin were looking at a full-page ad for Robin's business that also congratulated Morgan and the rest of the student musicians in the evening's recital. Robin had been able to make a $500 donation for taking out the ad, which was more than the regular advertising rate, but her business was doing so well that she could afford it.

"I'm glad I could do it. It feels good to be at the point where we can afford to make donations," said Robin, smiling and tapping the page in the program. "Who knows if we ever would have been at the point where we not only felt confident about paying for our kids' college, but also about making charitable donations."

"Not to mention feeling confident about our retirement," added Roy.

"And knowing that if anything comes up in life our financial plan will be flexible enough to handle it," Robin concluded. "I feel like it was just yesterday that we were going over these things with Jay and Brian for the first time. Now I feel like we're experts on the subject too." She laughed.

Just then Jack returned with several soft pretzels and two cans of soda. He squeezed his way down the aisle towards Roy and Robin. "There he is," said Roy. "I thought you'd forgotten all about us."

Jack plopped down into the seat next to Roy and sighed. "Boy, I tell ya," he said, handing a can of soda to his father. "Why didn't the senior girls look like this when I was in school?"

"My son, the ladies' man," snorted Roy. He examined the can that Jack had given him. "This isn't diet! I told you to grab me a diet soda."

Jack was munching on one of the pretzels and busily scanning the crowd for more females. "Sorry Pops. Was a little distracted."

"Geez, ya think!" said Roy, grabbing one of the pretzels away from his son before he could devour them all. "I just hope you pay this much attention to your class work! We're paying for you to study, not to watch the co-eds!"

October 12, 1994 (five years earlier)

"What are we going to cover today?" asked Robin, as she and Roy sat down at the table in Jay and Brian's office.

Jay laughed. "You're getting right down to business, aren't you? Don't you even want some coffee?"

"I could use some," said Roy. "After a cuppa joe I might be as wide awake as Robin." He winked at her.

Brian poured coffee from a carafe into four mugs. "Today we'll be going over The Financial Independence Expander. We're going to see what your retirement or financial independence looks like," he explained.

"If you remember, at the Blueprint meeting, you said you wanted to be financially independent by the age of 55," said Jay, as Brian slid the Sewells' Blueprint to him. "Your personal vision of financial independence is that your children's college education has been covered, you have your vacation property, you can take a great vacation every year and your portfolio is generating $75,000 per year for the rest of your life."

"That sounds about right," said Robin.

"Are we there yet?" asked Roy jokingly, stirring sugar into his coffee.

"Not quite," said Jay with a smile, "but you are definitely on track. Let's review what we accomplished so far." He opened the file in front of him and showed it to Roy and Robin, who both leaned forward for a closer look.

"We developed an action plan that will allow you to redo your kitchen and cover the children's private high school," Brian started.

"We're redoing the kitchen?" asked Roy in surprise.

"Yes, remember?" chided Robin. "That was my contribution to the Blueprint."

"Apparently," said Roy, sipping from his mug, his eyebrows raised. "Cause I certainly don't remember that one."

"A redone kitchen means I'm more likely to spend time in there helping Morgan bake cookies," said Robin.

"Like I'd said, a new kitchen sounds great to me!" deadpanned Roy.

"Sounds like you're all making out on that end of the deal," Brian smiled. He pointed to another spot in the file. "We also got you two started on a college savings plan, and you are saving $1,000 per month to it. You're also saving another $900 per month to the asset allocation portfolio we developed for you and you continue to maximize your 401(k) contributions. The Cash Flow Optimizer has helped you implement a savings strategy of almost $35,000 per year."

Roy let out a whistle. "That's unbelievable!" said Robin. "I knew the money should be there, but it seemed like we always managed to spend it before we could save it. It's amazing how much we really have when we don't fritter it away."

"We know, it is a problem that plagues most families," said Jay. "So as you can see, you are definitely on track for your vision of financial independence."

"Let's go over the numbers," said Brian. "Most people never undertake this exercise because it seems too far away or too hard. In reality, it's actually pretty easy." He turned to another page in the file and handed a copy of the page to both Robin and Roy to look at. "We took your budget from the Cash Flow Optimizer to project what your living expenses will look like in 10 years. Most people forget about inflation. The long-term inflation rate is 3%, which is what we use."

"What that means is that the $75,000 living expenses you have today will be over $110,000 ten years from today," explained Jay.

"The actuaries tell us you are going to live to be 85," Brian continued.

"How nice of them," said Robin. "Can they predict what we'll look like then?"

"We plug in the expected long-term growth rate for your investment portfolio, after fees, which is 8% in your case. This shows us the amount your portfolio needs to be to generate $110,000 in 10 years through your 85th birthday," Brian explained.

"We'll have to have a big party then," said Roy, pouring himself another cup of coffee. "If we can even stand by that age."

"I have a feeling we'll be doing okay," smiled Robin.

Jay flipped to another page in the file. "Another area that people forget is to back down the expected return of the portfolio when you retire or achieve financial independence. Remember that until retirement, growth is the main objective of the portfolio. Then, during retirement, income becomes the main objective and growth is second. We reduced the return to 6% at retirement."

"And yet another area people forget to consider is the taxes," Brian picked up. "Most people have the ability to pay taxes from current income until they retire. However, at retirement, it's a different story. You'll need to use the portfolio to pay taxes if it is your primary source of income."

"We used a 30% tax rate, which is a blended ordinary income and capital gains rate," Jay explained, handing the Sewells another sheet of paper to look at. "Afterwards, we plug all this into The Financial Independence Expander and get the result you'll need to accumulate approximately $3 million in 10 years."

"$3 million? That sounds like a lot!" exclaimed Robin.

"Looks like we can stop buying lotto tickets, honey," joked Roy.

"Think about it in simple numbers. If you can earn 6% on a $3 million portfolio then you will generate $180,000 per year. This is about what you need to cover your living expenses, taxes, and your vacations when you are 55, after taking inflation into account," said Jay.

"Math was never my forte, but it makes sense to me," said Roy. "So will our current savings plan get us to this point that you're talking about?"

"Yes it will," Brian affirmed. "But one thing you have to keep in mind is that you won't be able to save $35,000 every year, especially when the kids are in college."

"Oh boy," groaned Roy. "College. Why didn't anyone tell us how much kids were going to cost? If I'd known, I think I would have suggested getting a dog instead."

Jay laughed. "Well, taking the long-term expense of kids into account, we need to constantly monitor your cash flow so when extra money is available through bonuses and stock options you can save it."

"Speaking of stock options, I didn't see them on our Net Worth Statement. Did you miss them?" asked Roy.

"No," said Jay. "We don't consider unexercised options in The Financial Independence Expander. Stock options that are 'out of the money' are really a wild card. If they take off, you will be able to achieve your goals earlier than expected, or you can use the proceeds to start the family legacy and take care of the grandchildren's education."

"What does 'out of the money' mean exactly?" asked Robin in confusion.

Brian answered her. "It is when the exercise price, or the price at which you can buy the shares, is above the current market price. It wouldn't make sense to exercise options that are out of the money when you can buy the stock cheaper in the open market."

"I see," said Roy. "Grandchildren's education. That means paying for even more kids. Sounds terrific."

"What's your firm's position on social security?" asked Robin.

Jay smiled. "You're one smart cookie. I can see why Roy married you. As you can see, we use it in your cash flow projections as a source of income for you in retirement."

"We feel that social security will be available for you but it should not be relied upon," Brian added. "It's better to err on the side of conservatism. If achieving your goals is contingent on social security, we feel that is running it too tight and we would look to make some modifications."

"Good," said Robin. "I like that approach."

"Now keep in mind that these projections assume you achieve the long-term rates of returns we are expecting," Jay continued. "A major weakness in most financial planning software is that it assumes you earn those returns evenly every year. We all know that the financial markets don't work like that over the short-term. But they do over the long-term. So another analysis we perform during The Financial Independence Expander is what is called 'Monte Carlo Simulation'."

"Which is?" asked Roy.

"The simulation we're talking about here doesn't involve any screams and it keeps both your feet on the ground, so hopefully we won't have to worry about motion sickness," Jay smiled. "What we do is run over a thousand simulations of possible outcomes that your portfolio can experience over different time frames and the probability that you will meet your goals—in other words, have money left when you die—is calculated."

"Doesn't quite sound like a roller coaster," said Roy.

"Our minimum probability is 85% for us to accept the results," said Jay.

"How did we do?" asked Robin.

"You got a 93%," answered Brian.

"Do you think that's high enough?" asked Roy.

"Anything over 90% is a great outcome."

"Good," said Roy. He paused to sip his coffee. "But what about the concept that you should die broke that I read about?"

"That concept is really a misnomer," stated Jay. "What that concept really means is that you shouldn't give any money to Uncle Sam in the form of estate taxes when you die. We'll see to that during The Estate Planner."

"I should have known you guys would have it covered," laughed Roy. "Just goes to show you can't believe everything that you read. What's next?"

"Well," Jay said, "obviously the results of The Financial Independence Expander are very good. But keep in mind, there are still many unknowns that could wreak havoc on your goals. This is why once we develop the Financial Independence Expander, we have to constantly monitor and evaluate it to ensure that we are still on track."

"For example, a serious illness in the family can really throw off your plan," explained Brian. "So even though you're in good shape now, we can't rest on our laurels. Always remember that financial planning is a dynamic, fluid process. Life moves on and any good financial plan needs to keep up with it. That's why flexibility is key." He poured himself a bit more coffee and stirred in some creamer before continuing. "In our years doing this, we've seen too many financial plans developed only to sit on shelves for years, rather than being kept up-to-date. Plans like this give people a false sense of security. They don't realize how important it is to have a plan that grows and changes with them."

"Fortunately, the performance of the stock market has been really helping people, though it may be paralyzing them into not saving enough. We don't want this to happen to you. So always keep in mind that any good financial plan should expect change and have a process to deal with these changes and continue to move ahead," said Jay.

"So," Robin said, examining the papers in front of her. "I see that down the road, you have me starting my own business with the start-up capital. Where did that come from, our portfolio?"

"Well, we will have several options when the time comes to fund the start-up of the business. In the meantime, we want you to continue to fund according to plan," said Brian.

"Another point worth mentioning is that there is a great tug-of-war between short-term goals and long-term goals," said Jay, getting up to open the blinds covering the office windows. "The most obvious of these is college education versus retirement. We see so many people raid their retirement accounts to pay for their children's education. Generally, this is a big mistake."

"No kidding!" said Roy. "I need to make sure I'm taken care of financially when I'm old and gray."

"If you haven't set aside funds to cover your children's college education, then paying for it becomes a cash flow problem. We call this 'The Great American Irony'," said Jay.

"I'm a sucker for irony," said Roy. "Tell us more."

"Let's look at the typical American family," Jay said, sitting back down. "At age 48 most families have at least one child in college and one a few years away. Borrowing from the 401(k) to pay for college takes the money out of your investments in the form of a loan. Sure, you pay yourself back with interest. But what you lose is the opportunity for tax-deferred compound growth. And that is the key to the power of the retirement plans. So borrowing from your 401(k) defeats its biggest benefit."

"And most people don't realize this?" asked Roy. Jay shook his head. "Boy, we're sure lucky that *you* guys know this!"

"Say you have two kids and that you did have to borrow from your 401(k), draining your taxable accounts and savings," Brian picked up. "Your second child will be out of school when you are around 55. This leaves you about 10 years away from normal retirement age. So all the tax-deferred compound growth up to this point is gone forever. You can never get these years back. People need to figure out another way to pay for college. In our view, retirement accounts are not an option. We are extremely opposed to borrowing from the 401(k) for these reasons."

"So what are the options?" asked Robin.

"Apply for aid, take student loans, partner with your children, asking them to work on breaks and during the summer. Again, it's a cash flow issue and you cannot jeopardize your financial independence to get your children through college—unless, of course, you are willing to work an extra ten to 15 years," said Jay with a sly grin.

"No way!" exclaimed Roy. "Student loan city, here we come. And those kids better not think summer is playtime. They'll be working if I have anything to say about it!"

"You always do," Robin winked at him. "Fortunately we've got good kids and even at this young age they've got quite a work ethic. They always do their chores to earn their weekly allowance, and they're not too bad at saving even a little of it. So I think we'll manage, without having to drain our retirement away."

"Speaking of 401(k) accounts, when we retire, we'll have a lot of money in retirement accounts. What do we do with these accounts?" asked Roy.

"Well, you have several payout options," answered Brian. "You can annuitize your account which would guarantee fixed payments over different time periods. You could roll it over to an IRA. You could leave it in the 401(k) account if the company's plan allows this. There is no right or wrong answer. You really have to evaluate your need at retirement and determine the most tax-efficient use of your different buckets of money."

"And I'm guessing you'll help us determine this?" asked Roy.

"Absolutely," said Brian. "That's what we're here for."

"Remember, when you start withdrawing from your 401(k) accounts, the money is taxable to you," said Jay, folding his hands over his chest and leaning back in his chair. "I hear so many blanket answers about whether the right decision is to take all the money first, or wait until the end. All we can say is that it really depends on your cash flow needs and your tax bracket at retirement." He leaned forward again and re-crossed his hands on the table. "For instance, you may not need your IRA money so it could be an asset that you pass down to the next generation. The IRS, however, requires you to take minimum distributions after you turn 70 ½ years old. There are certain techniques to stretch the payment out over a long time in order to lower the required minimum distributions."

"Like I said earlier, this is something we will look at when you're closer to retirement," said Brian.

"Let's hope that comes sooner rather than later!" said Roy. "I have a question. Is there a time when it makes sense to stop making contributions to the 401(k)?"

"No," said Jay quickly. "Definitely not. Between the tax benefits and the company match, it is still the best tax-deferred vehicle to fund. In addition, with proper planning, you should be in a lower tax bracket at retirement so the money will be withdrawn at a lower tax rate."

"So the bottom line is to keep on maximizing our 401(k) contributions," said Roy. Jay nodded. "Boy, I'm a fast learner, aren't I?"

"Is there anything else we should be doing to stay on track for retirement?" asked Robin.

"You're both doing well at the moment. So just keep up what you're doing and be sure to enjoy life," said Jay. "So many people sacrifice their current lives worried about retirement. On the other extreme, so many people overspend and don't worry at all about retirement. It's the sad truth that most American families fall into the second category."

"Unfortunately, these families have no control over retirement," Brian picked up. "Retirement will be whatever they can afford, mainly from social security. People have to sacrifice a lot under this scenario. The Progression of Wealth Process allows you to take control of retirement. You get to call the shots, not the other way around. So as long as you continue what you're currently doing and as long as you can continue to meet your savings goals, you will stay on track," said Brian.

"Sounds good to us," said Robin, leaning back with a sigh of relief.

"It's amazing what a little advance planning will do to ease your life in the future," said Jay.

"You bet!" said Roy. "I'm feeling better about getting old and gray already. How about you, honey?"

"Well, I can't say that I'm thrilled about the gray part, but I think I can handle getting older," Robin said, arching a brow as she and Roy stood to shake hands with Jay and Brian. "Thanks again for the coffee, and for giving us so much peace of mind."

"Our pleasure," smiled Brian.

Later that evening, Roy came into their living room with a bottle of good red wine and two wine glasses.

"What's all this for?" asked Robin, setting down the book she had been reading.

Roy poured two glasses and handed one to her. "You heard what Jay and Brian said. Enjoy life! I figured we can enjoy life even in small ways. No need for a special occasion. We can break out the good wine just because."

Robin laughed and accepted the glass. "Roy, sometimes you're just too much!"

"Seriously. I know I was a skeptic going into this whole Progression of Wealth thing, but having someone help organize our financial life and set us on the right track to achieve our goals is very comforting. And it lets us enjoy the other parts of life, like this," Roy said, gesturing towards the bottle on the table.

"I used to worry about overspending and not saving enough money," he continued. "It's great to see that we're a lot better off than we thought. It feels like the weight is lifting off my shoulders."

"I know what you mean. I feel the same way," Robin agreed. "I feel like we've got a good plan in place to meet our goals and take care of ourselves and the kids and that's very comforting. We're certainly not going into it blind, and that's a big comfort."

The two clinked glasses and took a sip. "That's good wine," said Roy, picking up the bottle again to examine the label.

"Yes, it reminds me of that French restaurant in the city that we used to go to," said Robin, taking another sip.

"Let's see if your mom and dad can watch the kids on Saturday night," said Roy. "We should treat ourselves to a nice dinner, to celebrate the good life that we're living now and will continue to live down the road."

"Sounds like a plan," said Robin with a smile. "Tomorrow you call and make the reservations and I'll call my folks. Deal?"

"Deal," Roy responded, smiling back. "Cheers!"

Chapter 6 Overview:
The Financial Independence Expander™

The Expander now takes what you've learned from working on the other stages, pulls it all together into what the expected outcome will be, broken down by time periods so that not only will you know whether you will achieve your goals but you'll have a benchmark to work with and check against each year to see if you're on track. The remaining stages deal with items that people are not always so fond of but have to do anyway. Accumulation of wealth is fun. Protecting wealth is not so much fun but it needs to be done, because in life there are risks and you need to cover those risks.

Chapter 7

THE WEALTH PROTECTOR

"Some of it's magic, some of it's tragic,
but I had a good life all the way."

—Jimmy Buffet

June 19, 1998

ROBIN GLANCED AT HER SON JACK over the catalogues stacked before her
on the kitchen table. She and Morgan were reviewing colleges and Jack
was home from Villanova for the weekend. She knew Jack was eyeballing the
fridge and she didn't want him making a mess. She turned her thoughts to
Morgan. "How are you making out over there, honey?"

Morgan exhaled, rolling her eyes at the same time. "I think I'm going
blind from looking at all this glossy paper. Everything is starting to look the
same. I'm starting to think everything is!"

"Don't get discouraged yet," Robin said. "No one ever said this process was
going to be easy. Just stick with it." Spread out over the kitchen table were
colorful college catalogues, one or two of which were arriving in the mail almost every day. Morgan would be a senior in high school this fall, and since
the last time she had taken the SAT's in April, their mailbox had become a
popular place for college admission boards to send their wares. It didn't hurt
that she had done okay on her SATs, had good grades, and was involved in
numerous extra-curricular activities. Co-captain of the school band, captain of the lacrosse team, and student body treasurer—if all went well she
could get into a great school. Now the two of them were settling down to

select a list of schools Morgan was most interested in, to plan campus visits, interviews, and begin filling out applications.

Jack had made his way to the fridge and was busy foraging.

"Mom, make him go away," Morgan groaned. "I can't hear myself think with him around."

Robin turned to her son. "Jack, go away. We're busy."

"Augh, I think my brain needs some fuel, too. How 'bout it, Mom? Want me to fix us a snack? Nachos? Pizza bagels? A two-foot hoagie?" He looked at her with a mischievous grin.

"Let's not get carried away," said Robin. "This is a snack, not a three course meal! How about you fix us some of those pizza bagels for all of us— quietly? Those sound good." She watched him take a jar of tomato sauce and some cheese from the fridge. "Easy on the toppings for me," she cautioned, knowing Jack's tendency to prepare generous snacks.

"Does Villanova know how much it costs them to feed you?" Morgan chided. "I'm surprised you haven't eaten them out of a cafeteria yet."

Jack ignored her, busying himself with the snacks.

Morgan rolled her eyes. "He's already eaten us out of house and home. That's for sure."

Jack snorted. "No way. Mom and Dad could buy me truckloads of food a week and they'd still be fine," said Jack, placing the bagels in the toaster oven. "Mom and Dad seem pretty smart with their money."

"Well, we weren't always as smart as we are now," said Robin, thinking back to when she and Roy had first met with Jay and Brian. "It's just like school. You learn more every day, especially when you have the right teachers. And our guys down at HJ Financial happened to be the right teachers for us—with the right lesson plan. Speaking of which"—she tapped a catalogue in front of her and pointed to Morgan, who had edged over to see how the pizza bagels were coming along—"don't think you're off the hook for today just yet."

"I know," Morgan sighed again, dropping back into her chair. She stared at the stacks of catalogues in front of her. "There're so many of these that I barely know where to start."

"I know you'd rather be out with your friends today or driving to the shore, but we both agreed that since neither one of us was working today we'd try to make some headway with this." Robin glanced out the window. It was a beautiful Saturday afternoon in mid-June, and though Morgan usually spent her weekends off from her summer job down at the New Jersey shore with her friends, she had agreed to spend this weekend with Robin, getting a jump-start on her college search. "It's going to be a lot easier if you have someone with experience in this help guide you through the process. Remember, I went through the college application process myself."

Jack brought over a tray of bagels and set them down. "Yeah, but things have changed a lot since the Civil War, Ma. I'm sure the invention of the light bulb along the way has made things easier," Jack teased.

Robin tried to swat him with a rolled up catalogue and missed. "Just like your father. You're lucky you're out of arm's reach," she said. "Now quit fooling around. It's a lot easier if someone who's 'been there, done that' is there to help you through. Like when Jay and Brian helped your dad and me with our money. We had an idea of what to do, we just needed someone to guide us."

"So are we billionaires yet?" asked Morgan, putting the pizza bagels on her plate.

"We?" Robin asked with a sly grin, arching her eyebrows. "You got a mouse in your pocket? Who's we? If by 'we' you mean your dad and me, no. And if you mean yourself in that we, even more of a no. C'mon, let's get back to work." She held up a catalogue for Berkley. "How about this?"

Morgan wrinkled her nose as she bit into a bagel. "I don't think California is my scene."

"Okay," Robin tossed it into the "No" pile on the floor to her left. "This? Or this?" She held up Georgia Tech in one hand, and Duquesne in the other.

"Yes to Georgia Tech, maybe to Duquesne," said Morgan, patting her chin with a napkin. Robin divided them into piles accordingly. Later they would go through all the catalogues Morgan had selected and go over the admission guidelines, course offerings, and open house schedules. Robin had a planner ready to fill in with all the appropriate dates, as well as a stack of file folders in which to separate everything. She knew being so organized would help.

After sorting through all the catalogues and adding to Morgan's growing "Yes" pile, which included schools like Virginia, Villanova, Susquehanna, and Penn State, Robin was pleased at the quality of the schools she was choosing. She was even more pleased that she and Roy would be able to afford sending her to any school she chose.

She thought back years ago, when she and Roy started working with Jay and Brian on The Progression of Wealth Process. One of their big concerns was having enough money saved by the time Jack and Morgan were ready to go off to college to help them pay for their education, but also, not depleting their savings so much that none of it could go towards retirement. There had also been a concern about Robin's parents, who did not have a long-term care insurance plan. Though both were still fairly healthy at the time, Robin knew anything could come up at any time—and in fact it had. Her mother had been diagnosed with Alzheimer's disease a few years ago. The thought of sending her wonderful, sociable, and otherwise healthy mother to a nursing home, which would be the option with Medicaid, devastated Robin. She hadn't known how to care for her parents without draining their assets and her and Roy's own—until Jay and Brian had suggested long term care insurance, both for Robin's parents and eventually for themselves.

Just then, Roy walked into the room. "How goes the college search?" he asked, opening the fridge to pour some soda.

"Oh, it's going." Robin gestured to the piles around her. Morgan got up to look through the fridge for a Diet Coke. Jack's mouth was too full of a third pizza bagel, so he simply nodded.

"Great, glad to see you're making some progress. Or at least I'm assuming this mess is progress." Roy glanced at one of the catalogues. "'Nova, eh? Who's going to help you out with paying for that one?" he teased.

Morgan ignored him—she was an expert at it. Jack, still chewing, smiled and pointed at his dad. "You, Big Guy."

"Mm-hmm." Roy turned to Robin. "Oh, honey, I meant to ask you—how's your mom doing?" Roy asked, moving some catalogues and sitting down at the table.

"Well, Dad just called today. He said the nurses and caretakers that come in are all great. Someone is there 24 hours a day to help out with Mom, make sure that she is getting all the help and medications that she needs, and also to help Dad out with any errands or concerns. I'm so glad we were able to keep them both out of a nursing home. They love that house—they've lived in it since my sisters and I were all kids—and I know it means a lot to both of them that they were able to stay there and be taken care of at home. Dad says that even on her worst days, Mom will still perk up at seeing the garden out back that's been there since before I was born, and at having all those familiar photos around."

"That's great," said Roy. "I'm just hoping our kids are as smart and help keep *us* out of a nursing home!"

"Are you kidding? I'll be running circles around everyone else when I'm Mom's age," said Robin.

"In any case, we'll have the protection we need to keep you from running those circles around a nursing home staff," said Roy.

"I'm so glad Jay and Brian told us how to protect all the assets we worked so hard to gain and organize," said Robin, watching Jack push back his chair and deposit his plate in the sink. "Hey, buddy, you still live under this roof, so you better rinse that and put it in the dishwasher."

Jack made a face. "When I get rich someday, I'm going to hire people to do this for me," he said, turning on the faucet.

Roy grinned at Robin. "You just better hope you've got the right person around to show you how to get to the point where you *can* hire someone to do it for you."

"Oh, come on," said Jack, elbowing Morgan. "Aren't you going to leave us millions in your Will?"

"At the rate you're going, you better hope you even make it out the door, Mr. Smarty Pants!" said Robin, rolling up another catalogue.

"Well," said Roy, taking the catalogue from Robin's hand and unrolling it, "if nothing else, we should call to let them know that the Wealth Protector has gotten us to this point in our lives: where we don't have to worry about losing anything we've worked so hard to gain."

November 20, 1994 (four years earlier)

"What's the matter, Robin? You seem a bit distracted today," Brian asked as Robin and Roy sat down at the table in his office.

Robin sighed. "It's my mom. Lately she's been acting sort of scatterbrained. Like I'll call her and tell her Jack hit a home run in a game and it'll take her a moment to even remember who Jack is. And of course, forget about her even remembering the fact that he hit a homer." She rubbed her temples. "I know people's memories aren't as sharp when they start getting on in years, but this doesn't seem normal."

"Has your mother been to the doctor's recently?" asked Brian, his face registering concern.

"Yes, but he hasn't found anything really wrong with her. Maybe it's just a sign that she's getting old."

"Maybe," Brian agreed, "but you should definitely keep an eye on that in case it gets any worse."

"Gives us something to look forward to in our old age, huh?" asked Roy, with a sly grin. "Not even remembering your grandkids' names. Wearing an adult diaper. Getting stuck in some nursing home where everyone forgets to visit you."

"Well, that last part is only if you aren't careful," said Jay, who had walked in just in time to hear Roy's comments. He walked over to the table and shook hands with the Sewells. "It's never a fun thing to think about, but a lot of times these situations in life can be eased if you plan for them in advance."

"Plan for what, exactly?" asked Robin.

"Plan for the unexpected," said Jay.

Robin uttered a dry laugh. "But isn't that contradictory? How can you plan for something unplanned?"

"What Jay means isn't necessarily planning per se, but more like preparedness," Brian explained. "Sometimes life doesn't take the direction you'd originally planned. Things could happen, like disabilities that keep you from working or from taking care of your family, and this means that your ability to make income—an ability you'd once taken for granted—is suddenly gone."

"Remember when we were working on your Blueprint?" Jay asked. Roy and Robin both nodded. "We talked a bit about risks to the goals you laid out in the Blueprint. The main ones were losing your money, being unable to sustain your lifestyle, and being unable to achieve your goals. We need to make sure that no matter what happens, these risks do not debilitate your finances."

"That's right," said Brian. "This part of the Progression of Wealth Process is called the Wealth Protector."

"Sounds good to me," said Roy. Robin nodded. "We don't want to put in all this hard work just to have it eliminated by one unexpected incident."

"Everything valuable needs protection," Jay explained. "I wouldn't put a million dollar picture on display in a museum unless I knew the museum had a good security system to protect it from possible burglaries. I also wouldn't want to display it there unless I knew the museum was insured against any unforeseen emergencies, like fires or floods. In essence, that's what The Wealth Protector is. A security system protecting your valuables—though in this case, your valuables are primarily your loved ones and your assets. And the forces you are protecting them against are disabilities you may suffer, emergencies or property losses that are outside of your control, or even—God forbid—premature death."

"Right," said Roy. "Not exactly a cheerful topic, but it makes sense. So what do we do to make sure that we're protected?"

"Well," answered Jay, "we performed a needs analysis of what would happen if you lost the wages of a primary wage earner. In this case, both of you. Since achieving all your goals is contingent upon you meeting your savings goals and the long-term growth of your investment portfolio, the loss of one of your incomes would be devastating to the progression of your wealth. Our needs analysis looks at six major risks." He handed the Sewells a sheet of paper and read it aloud.

1) Premature death of a spouse
2) Disability of a wage earner
3) Personal liability lawsuit
4) Property damage or loss
5) Long-term sickness of a family member
6) Death taxes

"Geez," said Roy, "I was only really thinking about the first one."

"Yep, that's the one most people are familiar with," said Jay, nodding. "However, each of the six risks present their own unique challenges and can affect your financial independence very differently but in equally devastating ways. Let's discuss each one of these as they apply to your situation. We have reviewed all the coverage that you have in place, including your benefits at work."

"We prepared a survivor needs analysis to determine the amount of life insurance you need to have on each of your lives," Brian picked up. "In order to accomplish all the goals you have on your blueprint you need $2.5 million of insurance coverage on Roy and $1 million on Robin.

"Wow! Never knew I was worth that much!" exclaimed Roy. "It seems like a lot. How did you come up with these amounts?"

"It's simple. We just plotted all your future cash flows over both your lifetimes and did a present value calculation to determined in today's dollars how much money you each would need," said Brian. Robin and Roy looked at each other in confusion.

Jay jumped in. "Brian always makes it sound simple. It is a very complicated model that does this, but let me break it down in plain English. There are a couple of rules of thumb that you may have heard, but be careful using them because they don't take individual circumstances into consideration. Anyhow, a popular rule of thumb is that to retire and educate a child through college you need at a minimum $1 million dollars in life insurance. If you think about it, if you can earn 5% on the $1 million you could generate $50,000 in income each year. As you can see, $1 million in insurance doesn't allow for that great a life and it doesn't help you achieve any additional goals. So we are definitely not fans of rules of thumb. That's why The Wealth Protector goes through such a thorough insurance needs analysis."

Roy nodded. "Now I see what you mean. No wonder I'm worth so much."

"Another consideration is that the spouse who is primarily responsible for the kids and the house may not go back to work for at least several years, maybe not at all. The other side of this is that the primary wage earner will have to hire someone full time to assist with the kids and managing the house. So these needs have to be built into any sound insurance protection program," said Jay.

"I agree with what you're saying but I really don't like insurance," replied Roy. "I don't want to be insurance rich and cash poor."

"Well, think of it this way. No one likes to buy insurance and we really don't enjoy recommending it. It is a morbid subject and it is an additional cost," answered Jay. "The amount of insurance you need is not negotiable, however. Maybe the type of insurance is, but not how much you need."

"I guess you're right," said Roy.

"The thing is, we don't know too much about insurance," said Robin. "What do you mean when you say type? Wouldn't Roy just increase his coverage through work? Or couldn't we just call our car insurance agent?"

"No to both of those," said Brian. "The problem with work policies are that they are only good as long as you work there. It is much better to have a combination of both work and personal policies. And as far as the car insurance agent is concerned, you have to be careful. Not all insurance companies are created equal and not everyone is competitive in all types of insurance. What we do is shop the polices around but only with highly rated insurance companies. You could probably get a cheaper price from a lower rated insurance company but if that company runs into financial trouble they might not be able to pay death benefits to their policyholders."

"Why does it all have to be so complicated?" asked Robin in frustration.

"Well," said Jay, "with a lot of choices come complications. We work with an insurance specialist who provides us advice on the strength of insurance companies as well as the pluses and minuses of the various insurance products available. This helps us ensure that we can select the best product at the best price that will meet our clients' unique needs."

"Good," said Robin, leaning back, relieved. "It's in your hands then."

"We'll take care of it for you," said Jay with a smile.

"What's the difference between term and permanent insurance?" asked Roy.

"Term insurance is really meant to cover a temporary need over a specific period of time. For your situation, you have an insurance need at least until the kids are out of college. So a 20-year term would make the most sense for you. Term is the cheapest way to cover the need."

"Cheap is good," said Roy nodding.

"Permanent insurance on the other hand protects you over your entire life," Brian picked up. "So if you have a permanent need or are concerned about future health issues, permanent insurance may have a place in your program. The downside is that this type of insurance is more costly than term and the funding commitment is much greater."

"Explain what you mean by funding commitment," said Robin.

"One of the main benefits of permanent insurance is that it builds up cash value on a tax-deferred basis. So if structured properly, you can access the cash value tax-free in the future if the need for insurance goes away. There are so many different kinds of life insurance and different benefit options that most people get paralyzed. The first and foremost point of insurance is admitting that there is a need and then seeking the advice of trusted advisors to pick the right types of insurance for you," said Brian.

"Unfortunately, people are either naïve or simply living in denial because we see so many families that have not protected their loved ones," announced Jay. "And the excuse that 'It won't happen to me' doesn't cut it. Not to get on a soapbox here or anything," he said hastily.

"No worries," said Roy. "It makes sense. And it's a saying we all trick ourselves into using. Always good to remind ourselves that it isn't true."

"The next step is to go through the medical underwriting process so we can determine the status of your health and then we can shop around for the best policy at the best price," said Jay.

"Sounds good to me," said Robin, as Roy nodded in agreement.

"The next risk is disability of a wage earner," continued Brian. "This is the same concept as life insurance, but since the loss of income may be temporary, disability insurance pays out a monthly benefit as long as you are disabled. The likelihood of becoming disabled is much greater than a sudden death. Since disability benefits are generally not taxable, you need to replace at least 60% of your income. So Roy should have coverage for at least $10,000 per month, which replaces your salary at $200,000 per year."

"Is this something I should have the business pay for?" asked Robin.

"You can pay it out of the business but you don't want to take a deduction for the expense on the business' books," warned Jay.

"Why not? Isn't that one of the benefits of having the business?" asked Robin.

"Usually yes," said Jay, "but in the case of disability insurance premiums, if a business takes an income tax deduction for them, then any disability payments are taxable to the recipient," said Jay.

"Oh, we definitely don't want that to happen," said Robin.

"Definitely not," said Roy. "We pay enough in taxes as it is."

"The next two risks kind of go together: protecting personal property and protecting against lawsuits," said Brian.

"They go together, huh?" quipped Roy.

"Believe it or not, they really do," said Jay. "You obviously need to protect your home from a catastrophic loss such as a fire. The key here is to make sure you have replacement value coverage, which you do. Also your automobile deductibles and limits look adequate. What we did not see is umbrella insurance, which is also called excess liability of catastrophe coverage. You should have $2,000,000 of umbrella coverage," said Jay.

"What's the point of this?" asked Roy.

"Well, it covers you in case of a lawsuit above your homeowners or auto limits. With two children that will both be driving around the same time, you have exposure if they get into an accident and someone sues you. This coverage also protects you if someone is injured on your property. It is easy to add this protection to your existing homeowner's policy and it is relatively inexpensive to have," said Brian.

Questions to ask when looking over your disability policy:

1 What is the definition of disability?
2 How much disability income will you receive?
3 Do you have the maximum amount of disability coverage and can you purchase more in the future as your income increases?
4 Does the policy clearly spell out the definition of disability? Certain policies allow disability coverage if you can't work in your occupation, and others basically do not pay if you still have the ability to work at any job, so be sure to check and see which kind you have.

Questions to ask when looking at your homeowner and automobile policies:

1 Do you have the proper coverage?
2 Have you renewed the coverage to take into account appreciation in your house?
3 Does your homeowner's policy include valuable items such as diamonds, artwork, or collectibles?
4 Have you added an umbrella policy to your existing homeowner's to cover catastrophic losses?

"Boy! I don't even want to think about the kids driving yet, let alone getting into accidents!" said Robin. "Let's definitely make sure we get this added on."

"So who's gonna teach them how to drive, honey?" teased Roy.

"The next to last major risk you face is the long-term sickness of a family member," said Jay. Robin looked noticeably upset.

"What is it?" Roy asked quietly.

"Oh, I'm still concerned about Mom, that's all," said Robin. "I don't understand. She was always sharp as a tack, and now..." Robin lifted her hands and let them fall into her lap. "I guess I just don't want to admit that the worst could happen."

Roy placed his hand gently on her shoulder. "Don't worry. We'll make sure she gets the best care she can. And no nursing home, I promise. We'll find a way to keep her out of one."

Robin tried to smile back. Just then, Brian chimed in. "I've got a sugges-tion for dealing with your parents, Robin."

"You mentioned during our blueprint meeting that your parents may not be able take care of themselves," said Jay.

"Yes," she said, shifting in her seat. "Mom and Dad are in their early seven-ties and don't currently have significant assets. They are both pretty healthy at the moment—physically, anyway. But I am worried that something could happen to them down the road—especially with the way Mom's been so forgetful lately—and that if that happens, they won't be able to afford to care for themselves. And we might not be able to either," she said, giving Roy a worried look.

"I understand your concern," said Jay. "Long term care can get very expen-sive if a person is trying to pay for it on their own. Say you're paying $200 a day for your care."

"Yow," said Roy. "That's a lot."

"It is—especially if you're paying that every day for ten years, or even for one year. That's over $60,000 a year, just in basic care needs. It doesn't take in other, non-care related expenses."

"And that's only assuming that one of your parents needed the care," added Brian. "If both of them needed the care, it would double that amount."

"Well, what is there to do to avoid this?" asked Robin. "We won't have the money to pay for their care if they need it, and neither will they, but I don't want them to have to rely on Medicaid. That means they'll almost certainly go to a nursing home, and I just couldn't let that happen to them." Her eyes welled up.

"I understand your concern, Robin," said Jay. "Obviously you want to make sure your loved ones get the best care available. In order to make sure that your parents don't just end up on Medicaid, I'd suggest that you look into purchasing long-term care insurance for your parents. You said they're both pretty healthy right now, and this would ensure that they are cared for in the future."

"So this insurance covers any sort of long term care they might need?" asked Roy.

"Yes, whether it's having caretakers come into their home or whatnot. It ensures that they are cared for comfortably in their own home or in other environments that are not nursing homes—which can often offer imper-sonal and less specialized treatment than a personal caretaker."

"That definitely sounds like a much better option for Mom and Dad," said Robin, the creases in her brow relaxing. "It's a relief to know that there's this option out there. It's certainly something we'll do for them."

"As long as your parents don't mind going for a doctor's exam, we should start the underwriting for them right away, said Jay.

"I can't imagine they would mind. It seems like they go to the doctor's more than the casinos," Roy joked.

"As it should be," said Robin. "I don't have a problem with them being that way. Do you think we should buy this insurance for ourselves?"

"Yes, but not just yet," said Jay. "I'd suggest you wait until you enter your fifties to invest in this for yourselves."

"Augh, you said the dreaded 'F' word," said Roy. "Fifty." Everyone laughed.

"The last type of risk is the estate tax—also known as the death tax," said Jay.

"Here's a new one," said Robin.

"What do you mean 'a new one'?" asked Roy. "Don't you remember the saying: The only thing that's certain in life is death taxes?"

"That's death AND taxes, Einstein," Robin teased.

"Whatever," said Roy. "You're the wordsmith in the family, not me."

"Death taxes are the portion that Uncle Sam takes when you pass away," said Jay.

"God!" said Roy. "That pesky Uncle won't even leave you alone after you're dead!"

"What we are talking about here is Estate Taxes," Jay explained. "Since you are in the early stages of your wealth accumulation, you do not need a major estate plan developed at this time. But there are things we need to do today to start the estate planning process in the right direction," said Brian.

"For instance, you mentioned you do not have a Will. This is something that you must get done immediately. At a minimum, we need to name guardians for your kids," said Jay.

"We know, the guardians have been a point of contention for us," said Robin.

Roy jumped in. "I don't see how we can burden others with our children when they have their own to raise, feed, and educate."

"That is a valid point," said Brian. "Most people fail to execute a Will for exactly the same reasons as you. But to make your decision easier, remember that we are putting life insurance in place to address the financial responsibility of caring for your children."

"I never thought about it that way," said Roy. "That really would take a big part of the burden away. Okay, we'll resolve the guardian issue. Anything else we should be doing?"

"Yep. We will want to make sure all your assets are titled properly and all your primary and contingent beneficiaries have been named," said Jay. "This allows the assets to pass directly according to your wishes without having to wait for the Will to go through probate."

"Also, we will review the ownership of your insurance policies," said Brian. "The objective is to keep the insurance proceeds out of your taxable estate as long as possible. There are trusts that can keep insurance proceeds out of your taxable estates permanently, but you don't have the need for these types of trusts just yet."

"We will have a more detailed estate planning discussion after you have accumulated more assets," said Jay.

"Sounds good. Do you have an attorney that can do our Wills for us?" asked Robin.

"They've got everything else, so I'm sure they do," said Roy. "Am I right?"

"Right," said Jay. "We work with attorneys who will help take care of it."

"So now that we've looked at all of our insurance needs and are ready to put The Wealth Protector into place, do we have to do anything else?" asked Robin.

"We will review your insurance program every year," said Jay. "You need to do this because sometimes things change. For instance, the cost of certain insurance continues to decrease mainly because people are living so much longer. So we will be sure to keep up to date with all your policies and keep aware of any changes."

"Also, as situations in your life change, so will some of your needs," Brian added. "For instance, after both your kids graduate from college and are out on their own, your need for life insurance isn't going to be as pressing, because they won't be dependents anymore. And as you hit your fifties, you'll be looking into getting long-term care insurance for yourselves."

"So as time progresses and our lives change, we just make sure all of our protection changes with us?" asked Robin.

"Exactly," said Jay. "It's like updating your computer every couple of years. You make sure that you get and understand the latest edition of things so that you are up-to-date, but you're basically still performing a lot of the same functions."

"This is a sort of revolving event," added Brian. "That's why The Progression of Wealth Process has no real end to it—because we need to continually assess your progress toward financial independence and refine the plan as your life changes."

"That sounds good," said Roy. "What sorts of things should we be expecting to come up in future sessions?"

"Well, one thing you'll certainly need to look at is Robin's succession plan for her business. This means how will you eventually leave your business? Who will you leave it to? And how will this transition happen?"

"Hmmm, good question," mused Roy. "I guess we never really gave that too much thought before."

"Exactly the reason why we're here," Robin reminded him. "We just weren't sure what sorts of questions we needed to be asking."

Smiling, Brian crossed over to a filing cabinet in the corner and took out a booklet. He put it on the table in front of Roy and Robin. "This is what we call The Progression of Wealth Process for the Business Owner ," he explained. "This booklet explains the unique business needs the owner faces and their impact on their financial independence."

"This might also change the Cash Flow Optimizer and generate another source of retirement income," added Jay, as he stood and poured everyone a glass of water from the pitcher on his desk.

"Yes, and at the time that you're making these transitions, you'll need to take a strong look at your current life insurance policies, because you might not need the same ones you had before," said Brian. "And if you have variable life insurance, you need to consider if you should still be accumulating dollars in there, or if you should use some of the build-up in cash values to pay the premiums, or if you should continue to use this as an accumulation vehicle."

Jay carried water glasses over to Robin and Roy. "That's a lot to think about," said Robin, accepting a glass from Jay and taking a sip.

"That's why we're here," said Brian.

"We won't still need disability insurance when we're retired, will we?" Roy wanted to know.

"No, it doesn't really make sense to have a disability policy in retirement years. In fact, most of them are cancelled by then," said Jay, crossing over to the desk to get the other two water glasses. "It will be replaced with long-term care insurance."

"That's what I figured. I just wanted to double check," said Roy, drinking from the glass in front of him.

"As you go through Stage 1, the savings years, Stage 2, the pre-retirement years, and Stage 3, which are actual retirement, your Wealth Protector will continue to change.

"What can we expect when we are ready for estate planning?" asked Robin.

"The primary purpose of The Estate Planner is to be sure that you and not the state direct how your assets are distributed," explained Brian. "Estate planning provides for family security, business succession, the management of your assets, the nomination of a guardian for your minor children, and also helps to plan or reduce the costs of probate later on."

"What's probate mean, exactly?" Robin wanted to know.

"Probate is the legal process of determining the validity of a Will and the competency of the deceased person when they were making that Will," Jay said.

"Sounds sort of like tricky business," said Roy.

"It can be. Many people like to avoid probate and probate is not necessary for assets that pass automatically under the terms of ownership or beneficiary designation," said Brian.

"For example," Jay picked up, "let's say a husband leaves all of his assets to his spouse and they are held in joint ownership. These assets will pass automatically to the spouse without the need for probate."

"Sounds a lot easier that way," said Roy.

"Yes," Jay agreed. "In an instance like the one I just described, which avoids the probate process, it avoids tying up assets in court. This is a good thing because probate permits a court of law to supervise or transfer the assets of the descendent to heirs and typically lasts for one year."

"In addition, attorney fees and court costs are very high and this becomes public information, which is often unwanted publicity," said Brian.

"There are many ways to avoid probate," said Jay. "However, just as joint tenancy has the advantage of the estate passing automatically to your surviving joint tenant, there may be some asset protectors that work against a person. The best thing to do in this case is that you have an attorney help you prepare a Will."

"Which we will help you coordinate, of course," said Brian. Roy nodded.

"We recommend that you review your estate planning documents every three to five years," said Jay, getting up and walking over to his desk. He picked up some papers and walked back to the table. "There are certain events that occur in life that mean it's time to sit down and review everything. Here's the checklist." He handed Roy and Robin each a copy of the following list.

Estate Planning Checklist

- Marriage
- Divorce
- Death of a spouse
- Substantial change in estate size
- Moving to another state or country
- Death of an executor, trustee,
  or guardian if appointed in the original Will
- Birth or adoption
- Serious illness of a family member
- New business or change of business interest
- Retirement
- Change of health
- Purchase of property in another state or country
- Changes in income tax and estate tax laws
- Problem child
- Aging parents
- Special needs child

Roy and Robin looked over the list for a minute. "So for instance, let's say one of these occurs," said Roy. "Then we'd come in here to make sure everything is updated?"

"Exactly," said Brian. "It's important that you keep us up-to-date on whether any of these events occur."

"For instance, let's keep our fingers crossed that this happens," said Robin, pointing to "New business" with a grin.

"Now let's take a look down the road ten or fifteen years," said Brian. "Your kids will both be out of school."

"Let's hope," said Roy, rolling his eyes.

"At that time, you should perform some major estate planning, meeting with us to draw up Wills, trusts, and beginning to reduce your estate."

"This is a fairly complicated process," said Jay. "To put it to you briefly and simply, what will happen is that you will set up credit shelter and irrevocable insurance trusts. This will help you reduce your taxable estate and provide liquidity if there are any estate taxes due. And of course once you hit retirement it will be time again to make more changes in your estate planning."

"Because of the heavy demand that is projected on the Social Security and Medicare system from aging baby boomers, we recommend that you plan out your estate while you're healthy. There has been talk about eventually repealing the estate tax as long as I can remember. We can only assume that estate tax laws will be here to stay. However, we must ensure we build flexibility into any estate plan that we develop," cautioned Brian.

"Right," said Roy. "And you'll show us how to do this?"

"Yes," said Brian. "As well as making sure that your children and grandchildren are properly taken care of in your Wills as well."

"Wow, he said the 'G' word," said Roy playfully, pretending to look faint.

"Yes, sometimes it's hard for me to even think past the kids getting through high school!" laughed Robin. "It seems like it's an eternity away."

"Well, time plays tricks on people, Robin, and it will be here sooner than you think," said Jay.

"The important thing to remember," said Brian, "is that once you've reached your golden years you should not, for any reason, allow your life's hard work be subject to unnecessary loss from taxation or mismanagement due to little or no planning."

"Plus, the last thing your family should have to deal with in a time of grief is being hit with the costs of legalities and family squabbling. This way, everything will be in place and everyone will have peace of mind."

"That definitely sounds like the way to go," said Roy. "Enjoying those golden years surrounded by gold." He leaned back and smiled.

Robin shook her head. "Well if not gold, then at least enough to provide for some good times," she said.

"Exactly," said Jay. "Proper planning today can insure not only that your personal wishes are satisfied, but also that your family remains as strong without you as they were with you."

Later at home that night, Roy gave Robin a list of potential guardians for their kids.

Robin glanced at it and arched an eyebrow. "Do you really think Arnold Palmer or Warren Buffet would agree to this?" she teased.

"Worth a shot," grinned Roy.

"Maybe we should talk about this seriously," she laughed. "Something tells me Arnie might not be too prompt returning our phone calls."

After a few minutes of discussion, they agreed that Roy's brother and sister-in-law were the best candidates for the job.

"Why don't you call them and invite them over for dinner next Saturday?" Robin suggested.

"Will do," said Roy, picking up the phone.

Roy dialed his brother's number. "Hey Rick, it's your big brother."

"Roy! Good to hear from you. How are ya?"

"Robin and I wanted you and your lovely wife to come over for dinner next Saturday."

"Hey, can't turn that down! What's for dinner, surf and turf? asked Rick.

"Yep, you guessed it—hamburgers by the pool," joked Roy.

Rick laughed. "Count us in."

"Hey, as a heads up, we do have a little business to conduct with you and Lori," warned Roy.

"Everything okay?" asked Rick.

"Yeah, everything's great, we're just getting our finances in order."

"Sounds thrilling!" said Rick. "Well, any business you have to discuss with us sounds that much more appealing if accompanied by dinner."

"I figured I'd be able to bribe you with food," laughed Roy.

"It runs in the family."

"Sure does."

"Want me to bring anything?" asked Rick.

"Maybe just some beer, or wine if you think Lori would want some of that instead," said Roy.

"Done and done. See ya Saturday, big brother," said Rick.

After Roy hung up the phone, Roy gave Robin a big hug. "It's all set. I'm so glad we'll finally get these Wills done."

"Me too," said Robin. "We put it off for so long it seemed overwhelming, but when Jay and Brian broke it down for us it was easy to move forward."

"Thank goodness someone out there's organized!" said Roy.

Chapter 7 Overview:
The Wealth Protector™

The Wealth Protector will analyze all the risks that you face and provide ways to control those risks. Although financial independence is a great goal, it can be taken away at any point. The purpose of The Progression of Wealth Process is that wealth is not just about money; it's about having a great life. The Wealth Protector assures that you've covered those risks so you do not have to worry and you can continue to have a great life.

The Estate Planner ensures an orderly and efficient transfer of your wealth according to your wishes. The Estate Planner enables you to maximize your estate for your beneficiaries by reducing the tax burden. In addition, The Estate Planner will make sure your Will is adequate, your assets and liabilities are correctly titled, and all your beneficiaries are designated.

Chapter 8

THE LOVED ONES' LETTER

"There are places I remember all my life,
though some have changed, some forever not for better,
some have gone and some remain."
– John Lennon / Paul McCartney

November 18, 2003

ROBIN LEANED BACK IN HER SEAT, pen in hand, gazing at the scenery around her. She and Roy were currently on a two-week trek across several European countries, but this was no college kid's backpacking hostel trip. Instead they were staying in fine hotels, enjoying gourmet meals, and spending each day sightseeing at different attractions and sampling a bit of local culture. The two had started out in Austria, then headed to France, and were currently in Spain before their final destination of Italy.

This was a trip for just the two of them, which Robin found immensely relaxing. Luckily, Morgan was bogged down with her graduate classes at Wharton and Jack was saving his vacation time to go running with the bulls in Pamplona this summer with a bunch of his friends.

It was nice to have time just with Roy again—especially since things were going so well in their lives. Her own business was booming, with two more new employees, rounding off the total to ten, and over thirty clients. Having so many people working for her meant she had a bit more time now to relax and enjoy being the boss—and this meant having more time to spend with Roy. It also meant the perk of being able to afford a wonderful vacation. Roy's company was doing well also, and this meant he was less stressed and far more cheerful. The time the family spent together was much more pleasant because none of it was devoted to financial woes and worries. Ever since Roy and Robin had started working with Jay and Brian on their Progression of Wealth plan, they had felt much more secure and confident about their finances, and this led to a lot less stress in all other aspects of their lives.

Robin continued surveying the sights around her on their third floor patio balcony as she sipped a light white wine from a glass on the table beside her. She and Roy were taking the afternoon to relax before going to a nearby restaurant that featured strolling Spanish guitarists and a flamenco dancing show. The afternoon was beautiful, and she was enjoying the breeze and sunshine. Just then, Roy walked out with his own wine glass.

"It's a gorgeous day out, huh honey?" he asked, strolling to the railing and looking out at the street scene below.

"Yes, we couldn't have asked for a prettier day," Robin agreed. "I'm so glad we decided to take this vacation. We've wanted to tour Europe for years, but we never thought we'd be able to."

"Oh, I know. I think we waited until just the right moment too. No offense to the kids, but this is much more relaxing without them!" he laughed, turning to face Robin.

She giggled. "Yes, great kids though they may be, it certainly makes it much easier to travel for two instead of four."

Roy walked over and sat in the chair beside Robin. "Ahh, it feels nice to just relax. We've been seeing so many sights lately, I needed to rest my eyes." He leaned back in the chair and closed his eyes. After a moment, he opened them again and glanced over at Robin, who had resumed writing. "What are you working on over there? Please tell me you haven't brought work with you to do."

Robin gave him a wry grin. "What do you take me for, a workaholic?"

"Maybe." Roy sipped at his wine.

"No way. I'm enjoying this vacation all the way. I've worked hard, and I deserve a break. I'm just making out some postcards for Dad and the kids." She held up the one she was working on. The front of it portrayed a flamboyantly dressed flamenco dancer.

"Woo, that's a lively card," said Roy. "Who's getting that one?"

"Jack," Robin laughed. "Of course."

"Of course," echoed Roy. "You do realize that we'll probably be home before these cards make it there."

"I know," said Robin. "But I still think it's important to send the people you care something to let them know you're thinking about them. Even if it gets to them late," she said, giving Roy a look.

"I guess you're right," said Roy, setting down his wine glass. "I always did like getting cards and notes from you and the kids. It does show that the other person is in your thoughts."

"Exactly," said Robin, putting the finishing touches on Jack's card. "Putting things in writing just seems to make them seem that much more sincere, because the person writing them is making the commitment to put the words down on paper." Finished with the message, she began to address the card.

"Yeah, you know what they say about the power of the written word," agreed Roy. "It makes things so much more permanent. It's like the Loved Ones' Letter that Jay and Brian have us update every few years."

"It's an important way to capture a person's wishes and have proof that it's what the person wanted," said Robin. "It makes it so much more permanent."

"I used to think that just a Will would do," said Roy. "But I'm glad Jay and Brian encouraged us to do this."

"Even if it was like pulling teeth to get you to do it!" said Robin.

Roy stood and finished the wine in his glass. "Hey, I'm not the writer in the family. Judging by the way you've been keeping yourself occupied all afternoon, it's certainly you who likes putting pen to paper." He started to head inside, then paused. "Maybe it's a reflection on how much you like to talk." He grinned playfully at her.

"You're just lucky I'm too relaxed to get up and come after you!" said Robin, laughing. She watched Roy retreat inside and thought about their Loved Ones' Letters that they had first written so long ago. It had been tricky at first but once they got into the swing of things, it was no problem to update their letters every couple of years.

As she finished her wine and finished up addressing Jack's postcard, she thought back on that meeting nine years ago and realized what a long way they'd come.

November 10, 1994 (nine years earlier)

"So, did you do your homework?" Jay asked Roy and Robin, sipping from his cup of coffee. He and Brian were sitting with Roy and Robin at a local coffee shop on a cool Saturday afternoon.

Roy laughed and leaned back in his chair. "No one told me the Progression of Wealth was going to be like being in school. I thought I was done with homework."

Brian laughed too. "Just wait till we start giving you pop quizzes!"

Robin leaned over and pulled some papers out of her bag. "Here's what we came up with," she said, handing a copy of the papers to both Jay and Brian.

Roy cleared his throat and looked over at Robin. "What exactly are we covering today?" Roy asked in a stage whisper.

Jay chuckled. "Aren't you lucky that Robin's on the ball?" he said, and winked at Robin. "During this stage we will go over The Loved Ones' Letter."

Roy smacked his forehead with his palm. "That's right! I knew that. It just slipped my mind."

"Sure it did," Robin teased.

"So refresh my memory," said Roy. "Why exactly do we need to have letters like this?"

"The Loved Ones' Letter ensures that the estate planning part of your wealth protector happens most effectively," Brian explained. "Each year, millions of dollars in assets revert to the state because heirs cannot find necessary documents and information. Many people keep important things hidden for security purposes, but the one thing that should never be hidden from your family is the Loved Ones' Letter. It's almost like a map telling them where to go to find everything they need to get to the 'treasure'—which in this case is your estate."

"If you ever had to arrange the finances for the estate of a loved one that passed away, you know how challenging it is at such an emotional time," said Jay. "We find time and time again that one spouse usually handles the finances and the other one has no idea.

These people invariably live in The Fragmented Finances Trap so at their death there is a paper jungle to deal with. It is very stressful and there is little way to know if you identified every account and every insurance policy," he explained.

"We think that the Loved Ones' Letter should be prepared at all stages of your Progression of Wealth, so you should update it every few years, or any time there are any major life changes that affect your Wealth Protector," Jay continued.

"We were pretty much able to use the same letter for both of you," Jay went on. "We will just make two copies of it and change the name at the top. So in this sample that we made for you, we pretended it was from Roy to Robin. There are copies of your important items checklists as well." He cleared his throat and began reading:

Dear Robin:

This letter is a reminder of all of the matters that we have talked about over the years. It should not be construed as my Will. A copy of my Will is in our safe deposit box at the PNC bank on the corner of Main Street and 6th Street, and a copy has also been furnished to our financial advisors, Jay Heller and Brian Kohute of HJ Financial Group. They will help advise you and select an attorney for the issues you will be facing during the next year. There is a file in our computer system that lists all of our investments called "Roy and Robin investments." A more accurate count is directly available from Jay Heller or Brian Kohute of HJ Financial Group.

I have attached to this Loved Ones' Letter a checklist that gives a full description of all of the advisors we currently use. However, once again through The Progression of Wealth Process™, HJ Financial Group handles all of this and has been furnished with a copy of this checklist as well as helping me to prepare the checklist and letter, which you are involved in. If for some reason Jay Heller is unable to assist you with the execution of our estate you can have his partner, Brian Kohute assist you.

The checklist also has a complete listing of all of our assets. I have included here only assets that are not supervised by HJ Financial Group, including our homes. However, they are fully aware of all of our assets except for a few stock certificates that I keep in our safe deposit box and some savings bonds that are attached to this list. In addition, we have no outstanding liabilities at this time except for some credit cards. You will need to make arrangements with the credit card companies to take me off the credit cards and put your name exclusively on them.

On the insurance coverage part of the list, I have

listed all of the insurance we have, but once again
HJ Financial Group has supervised the insurance
policies and has complete information on this. As
you know, when we reach 65 we will discontinue our
disability policies so that will not be on the list;
however, our long-term care insurance will be listed.
Once again, HJ Financial will have this information.
You will have to make arrangements with our health
insurance company to cancel my benefits. Remember to
submit to my employer the Certificate of Death. I have
also included a detail of all of the documents that
were signed and are all located in our safe deposit
box. HJ Financial Group, and our attorney, John
Smith, also hold copies.

For general information I have included, just to
make it easier for you, my social security, driver's
license, and passport numbers. A copy of my Will as
well as yours is located in our safe deposit box and
also held by HJ Financial Group and our attorney. I
have named you and our children Jack and Morgan as
co-executors of my estate and as such you will be
responsible for various duties which John Smith will
explain to you. Arrange to see John and Jay after
the funeral so that you can start the probate of the
Will without delay. Your income should be more than
accurate based on the Progression of Wealth planning;
however, once again these are events where you need
to redo the Progression of Wealth Blueprint and
the Progression of Wealth Process. You do not need
to rush into this; however, you should begin this
process within two months and I'm sure Jay or Brian
will contact you to do this. I do believe that you
and the children are adequately provided for and will
be well taken care of. The title to our homes is in
both of our names and will pass to you outside the
probate court. The deed is in our safe deposit box.

As far as my final wishes are concerned, I have
enclosed a checklist of those. Once again, I love you
and the children and hope that during this trying
time this letter makes it a little easier for you.

Love,
Roy

"This looks good," said Robin solemnly. "And I can see by the draft of the checklist you included [in Appendix D] that you've got all the important materials included."

"The Loved Ones' Letter at different stages will take different turns," Jay explained. "You may have a paragraph talking about such things as joint bank accounts. You may want to go into more detail as far as funeral and burial coverage. You may want to go into a lot of detail about your children's education or your wishes about how to raise them. You may even want to make a separate letter for each of your children."

"That's not a bad idea," mused Robin. "I know the kids know how much each of us cares about them and is proud of them, and how much we want for them, but it's always so validating to see someone you care about put their feelings for you down in writing."

"Yes," Roy nodded. "I guess it's a way for them to hold onto something."

"The Loved Ones' Letter is really just a supplement to the checklist and will certainly help your spouse get through a trying time," said Brian. "You should just remember that it isn't a substitute for a Will." Roy and Robin nodded.

"It isn't exactly a cheerful topic though, is it?" said Roy, drinking from his coffee cup. "I mean, all this thinking about what will happen after we die."

"Well, it may not be cheerful, but it is certainly important to be prepared for it," said Jay. "Spending a little time preparing for it now will prevent a lot of grief later."

"True," said Robin, nodding.

"So can we expect to look forward to even more cheerful topics next time we meet?" asked Roy with a wry grin.

"If you consider your taxes to be a joy, then yes you can," said Jay with a wink.

Roy laughed. "I can't wait!" he said, finishing his coffee and shaking the empty cup. "Looks like we'll need even more caffeine to get us through next time."

Chapter 8 Overview:
The Loved Ones' Letter™

The Loved Ones' Letter is another one of those tools that you put together and put away, but in case something happens to you or your spouse your family will be appropriately taken of. The Loved Ones' Letter is one of the easiest tools in the Progression of Wealth, but is often sometimes the hardest to complete because of its emotional subject matter.

Chapter 9

THE INCOME TAX STRATEGY

"I can see clearly now, the rain is gone;
I can see all obstacles in my way.
Gone are the dark clouds that had me blind;
it's gonna be a bright, bright shiny day."

– Johnny Nash

April 12, 2003

ROY PAUSED WITH HIS PAINTBRUSH IN THE AIR and inhaled deeply. The fresh salt air filled his lungs and the sun beat down warmly on his back. Even though it was only early April, it was quite warm out, and he was able to work comfortably in shorts and a T-shirt.

He was standing on the second floor balcony of a summer house he and Robin had recently purchased in Ocean City, New Jersey. They'd bought the house on the old "unique-fixer-upper premise" but the price was right and it was on the beach. It was a good place to call home for the summers of their retirement years. Still, it needed some work—like a fresh coat of paint to the deck. Roy knew he could afford almost any house they wanted—but Roy loved working with his hands and it was his house after all. He had the time. He'd do it himself.

Roy gazed out at the ocean view. He felt giddy about owning his first ever beach house. He had no notions of investing in real estate. But a summer house for Robin and the kids had always been a dream of Roy's.

Working steadily for 90 minutes or so, Roy took a break. He set down his paintbrush and walked to the other side of the balcony, which wrapped around three quarters of the second floor. Robin was there, fixing up some wooden patio furniture she had found second-hand.

"I can't believe we got this furniture so cheap," she said, looking up at Roy. She squinted in the sunlight. "All that was wrong with it is that it needed a new coat of paint and some of those decorative cushions to put on the seats."

"That's us," said Roy with a grin. "The perpetual bargain hunters. The eternally smart investors. How about we go in for something to drink?"

"Sounds good," said Robin, standing. "I'm getting thirsty."

They walked inside to the kitchen and Roy opened the cooler of drinks and snacks they had brought. He poured some lemonade into two plastic cups and handed one to Robin. "This house is really gonna be great when we're done, don't you think?"

Robin took a long swallow of lemonade before answering. "Yes, I think it will be a big hit with the kids. It's got plenty of space, and the big wrap-around deck, and it's even got a view of the ocean."

"Not to mention it's close to the boardwalk," said Roy. "I can't believe how lucky we were to find this house. You know a great house is almost impossible to find down at the Jersey shore."

"Oh, I know all right," said Robin. "You are a shrewd negotiator."

"Well, it just needed some work, that's all," said Robin. "And since we've got more time on the weekends now than most people, we'll surely get everything done in time for summer."

"Yeah," Roy agreed, finishing his drink and pouring a second one. "I can't believe how many people are cooped up inside today frantically trying to finish their tax returns."

"I'm glad we have someone to help us with our tax planning," said Robin. "Boy, things were a mess before that."

"Oh, definitely. Those frantic people cooped up on a gorgeous Saturday in April would have been us if we hadn't gotten all that helpful advice," agreed Roy.

"We wouldn't even have started thinking about acquiring a beach house if it hadn't been for the The Progression of Wealth Process," said Robin. "I'm so glad we finally have a good plan for our taxes."

"Yup. Remember how we just used to toss receipts into a shoebox and try to struggle with them two weeks before taxes were due?" Robin chuckled. "What were we ever thinking?"

"Apparently not much," said Robin. "I'm glad our financial advisors take care of everything—even our taxes."

Roy rummaged through the cooler. "Grapes? Apples? Are these the only snacks you packed, sweetie?"

Robin finished her lemonade and stood to go back outside. "They're healthy snacks. Someone should start watching their weight," she teased, walking up behind Roy and poking him in the stomach.

"Oh, so that's your game, you fiend. Besides, I do watch my weight!" said Roy, as Robin shook her head and walked back outside. "I just don't necessarily watch it go down all the time." He took out a grape. "Maybe I can pretend this is an M&M." He chewed, then frowned. "Nope. The Progression of Wealth may be magic to our finances, but it doesn't do the trick when it comes to turning grapes into chocolate!"

November 7, 1995 (eight years earlier)

It was a briskly cold November day as Roy and Robin entered the offices at HJ Financial Group. They sat across from Jay and Brian at their office conference room.

"Today, we want to review your tax position," said Jay.

"Aren't we about 6 months too early?" inquired Roy.

"No, we're right on time," answered Jay.

"Before we never ever thought about taxes until around March and then got serious around April 12th," said Robin.

"Yeah, the American Way," said Brian. "Why do today what you can put off until tomorrow. Unfortunately, if you follow that philosophy, you'll never get ahead financially."

"Let me explain," Jay said. "There are two parts to The Income Tax Strategy: planning and compliance. Most people understand the compliance part—you have to file your tax returns eventually each year but most people ignore the planning part."

"You guys love making us plan for things—now it's taxes," joked Roy.

"We can tell you story after story about clients paying thousands of dollars in taxes that could have been avoided with some proper planning," said Jay.

"Ouch," said Roy. "How did that happen?"

"Let's take a simple example. Say you have a beach house that you rent out most of the summer and you decide to sell the house and buy a newer, bigger one. If you sell the first house at a gain you will pay capital gains taxes on the profit. You may have been eligible to do a like-kind exchange and roll the gain of the first property into the new property and defer the capital gains tax until you dispose of the new beach house. Unfortunately, it is a relatively complicated transaction that must be structured just right. Once the new property is bought, however, there is little chance to qualify for like-kind exchange treatment. People need to recognize that they should speak to a CPA before they enter into transactions that may have tax consequences," Brian explained. "It's too late to plan after the transaction is completed."

"That makes sense." said Roy.

"Tax planning will be especially important once you launch your business, Robin. Then we will talk you through The Progression of Wealth Process for Business Owners™" *[See Appendix E for explanation of The Progression of Wealth Process for Business Owners.]*

"So this is why we do tax planning in November," said Brian. "We cannot plan to reduce your current year taxes in March or April of the following year. It's too late by then."

"To every question there is an answer," said Roy.

"So how do we reduce our taxes this year?" asked Robin.

"Good segue," said Jay. "We ran a tax projection based on your income earned to date as well as what you expect to earn through December."

"Do you know what Robin will earn the rest of the year?" asked Roy.

"Yet another benefit of HJ Financial Group—financial fortune telling!" laughed Robin. "Brian asked me for an estimate of my earnings for the year in October," she explained to Roy.

"Your expected liability is currently projected at $25,000," said Jay.

"How can this be?" asked Roy angrily. "Robin, have you been making the quarterly estimated payments?"

"Calm down," said Robin. "Jay and Brian send me vouchers and instructions each quarter, so yes, we paid in all the quarterly estimates. Let Jay finish explaining what is going on, Roy," said Robin.

"Sorry to break this to you, Roy, but the tax problem is due to the options you exercised and sold this year," said Jay.

"Oh boy," Roy groaned. "I guess you can use me as the example for your next client meeting."

"Yes, but as a good one," said Brian.

"How so?" asked Roy.

"Hey, it's November, not April, and you're in here working on this, so we still have time to plan to reduce this liability," said Brian.

"Phew!" said Roy. "That's a relief. So what do we need to do to get the liability down?"

"It's time to set up a retirement plan for the income Robin is earning part-time from her consulting business. Since you do not have any other employees at this time, we can make a contribution of $7,500 before tax this year by setting up a Simplified Employer Pension Plan, or SEP," Jay explained. "Since Robin currently works out of your home, we can also take a home office deduction. We can itemize all business-related expenses and we can allocate a portion of your home bills and depreciation for the part of the house that represents the home office."

"Wow, I didn't know we could do this," said Robin in amazement.

"You sure can," said Jay.

"We have reviewed your investment portfolio and you have significant losses in the discount brokerage accounts that we didn't transfer when we covered The Investment Portfolio Optimizer," explained Brian.

"Yeah all those stocks that Roy bought," said Robin.

"They'll come back" said Roy. "You just wait and see."

"That's what I've been doing for years," said Robin dryly.

"While I agree with Roy in theory, you have such a concentration in so few stocks that a large percentage of them may never come back. Our recommendation is to perform a tax reduction technique known as 'tax loss harvesting'," said Brian.

"How does this work?" asked Roy.

"Let me explain," answered Brian. "The sale of your options resulted in large capital gains because you have such a low cost basis in the stock."

"Yeah, but the stock was falling, so I wanted to cash some stock out," Roy said defensively.

"I understand," said Brian. "But now we need to address the tax consequences of the sale. We can sell your stocks and realize the losses to offset the capital gains you realized on the sale of your company stock," said Brian.

"I like the sound of that, but I don't want to be out of the market and miss any bounce and recovery," said Roy.

"We don't want you to be out of the market either. The other part of the tax loss harvesting strategy is to stay fully invested in the stock market. We do this through a diversified stock portfolio. The key to the technique is to buy similar but not identical stocks. There is a tax rule called 'wash sales.' The wash sale rule prevents people from selling a stock for a loss right before the year-end and then buying the stock right back. There is a 60 day window that prevents you from selling and buying the same stock," explained Brian.

"If we sell all the stocks that have losses, we can shelter all the capital gains on your company stock and also be able to reduce your ordinary income by $3,000. We will also have another $10,000 in capital loss carry forwards to reduce taxes in future years," stated Jay.

"Sounds good to me, but what will that do to our tax liability?" asked Roy.

"Here's the best part of all," said Jay. "If we employ the above recommendations, you will actually receive a $1,200 refund."

"Sign us up!" said Robin. "We don't want to have to pay."

"So how do you feel about everything we've gone over?" asked Jay.

"We definitely feel much more confident about everything involving our taxes," said Roy. "Before we were such a mess about everything. We didn't know how to keep anything organized or how to do our taxes to our greatest benefit. Now we feel a lot better, and you both gave us a lot of great advice."

"Yes," Robin agreed. "I have a feeling that this year when April 15th rolls around, we won't be pulling our hair out quite so much."

"Or not at all," said Jay. "The high anxiety that many people feel over their tax returns is something that doesn't fit into the Progression of Wealth. We try to make things so that you feel good about them and so that they cause you the minimal amount of worry. That's the whole purpose of the Progression of Wealth: knowing that your financial life is taken care so that you enjoy the rest of your life."

"It's definitely a good feeling," said Roy.

"The next step is the actual preparation of your tax return, which typically happens sometime between mid-February and April 15th," said Brian. "We'd recommend getting it done sooner rather than later."

"We'd also recommend letting us prepare your tax return," Jay added. "It goes with the whole idea of keeping stress at a minimum. We are CPAs, you know."

"But we've always done our own taxes," said Roy. "I thought that since the two of you had helped us with our year-end planning that we could just pick up one of those computer programs they have out now for doing your taxes yourself."

"Well, this is one route you could take," said Jay. "But it's very time-consuming and the one glitch is that tax laws are constantly changing."

"Here's a little crash history course," said Brian. "In 1913 the tax law was adopted, and there have been multiple changes every year since that time. That's a lot of changes. It just goes to show that it takes years and years of knowledge and being kept up-to-date with everything going on. That's why it's best to let us handle your taxes, especially if it's going to be a complicated return."

"Hmm," Roy mused. "I guess then it would be best for us to have someone like you to help us out."

Jay nodded. "Right. We'll provide you with a detailed checklist that will help you gather together all the information we will need. Then you simply gather it together and mail it to us, or you can come and meet us personally, like we're doing now."

"Gosh, that sounds a lot better than the way we were doing it before," said Roy. "Rushing to get everything done at the last minute and speeding to the post office the day our return is due. That was definitely awful."

"You'll certainly find that it will be better for you this way," said Jay. "If you do your taxes yourself instead of having a qualified professional do them, you risk losing a tremendous amount of opportunities. Plus, there are naturally advantages to having a CPA represent you if you have problems with the Internal Revenue Service or other taxing authorities."

Roy shuddered. "I bet there are."

"In your case, this just seems like the best way to go," Jay continued.

"And I think that once you get used to filling out that checklist of items that are needed for your taxes, it'll become like second nature to you," added Brian. "Here's a copy of it." He handed the Sewells a sheet of paper...

Checklist of Items Needed for Doing Your Taxes

Personal Data

- *Social Security Numbers (including spouse and children)*
- *Child care provider : Name, address, and tax I.D. or Social Security Number*
- *Alimony paid: Social Security Number*

Employment & Income Data

- *W-2 forms for this year*
- *Unemployment compensation: Forms 1099-G*
- *Miscellaneous income including rent: Forms 1099-MISC*
- *Partnership, S Corporation, & trust income: Schedules K-1*
- *Pensions and annuities: Forms 1099-R*
- *Social Security/RR1 benefits: Forms RRB-1099*
- *Alimony received*
- *Jury duty pay*
- *Gambling and lottery winning*
- *Prizes and awards*
- *Scholarships and fellowships*
- *State and local income tax refunds: Form 1099-G*

Homeowner/Renter Data

- *Residential address(es) for this year*
- *Mortgage interest: Form 1098*
- *Sale of your home or other real estate: Form 1099-S*
- *Second mortgage interest paid*
- *Real estate taxes paid*
- *Rent paid during tax year*
- *Moving expenses*

Financial Assets

- *Interest income statements: Form 1099-INT & 1099-OID*
- *Dividend income statements: Form 1099-DIV*
- *Proceeds from broker transactions: Form 1099-B*
- *Retirement plan distribution: Form 1099-R*

Financial Liabilities

- Auto loans and leases (account numbers and car value) if vehicle used for business
- Student loan interest paid
- Early withdrawal penalties on CDs and other time deposits

Expenses

- Gifts to charity (qualified written statement from charity for any single donations of $250 or more)
- Unreimbursed expenses related to volunteer work
- Unreimbursed expenses related to your job (travel expenses, uniforms, union dues, subscriptions)
- Investment expenses
- Job-hunting expenses
- Job-related education expenses
- Child care expenses
- Medical Savings Accounts
- Adoption expenses
- Alimony paid
- Tax return preparation expenses and fees

Self-employment Data

- Business income: Forms 1099-MISC and/or own records
- Partnership SE income: Schedules K-1
- Business-related expenses: Receipts, other documents & own records
- Farm-related expenses: Receipts, other documents & own records
- Employment taxes & other business taxes paid for current year:
- Payment records

Miscellaneous Tax Documents

- Federal, state & local estimated income tax paid for current year: Estimated tax vouchers, cancelled checks & other payment records
- IRA, Keogh and other retirement plan contributions: If self-employed, identify as for self or employees
- Records to document medical expenses
- Records to document casualty or theft losses
- Records for any other expenditures that may be deductible
- Records for any other revenue or sales of property that may be taxable or reportable

"I bet we could set up a filing system at home where we keep things organized as we go," said Robin.

"That sounds like a great idea," said Roy. "You'll just have to train me as to where things go. She's the super-organized one, not me," he explained to Jay and Brian. "Not to say that I'm not organized, of course. She's just better at setting up filing systems. She has a brain for that sort of thing."

"That is definitely a good idea," agreed Jay. "You two are starting to think more and more like us every day." Roy and Robin grinned.

"It's a good mindset to have," said Roy. "We're financially confident and comfortable now that we have someone to demystify things for us."

"And that means we have more time to concentrate on our kids and each other," said Robin. "I've noticed that ever since we started coming here and having our finances explained by the two of you, things have really started improving."

Brian smiled. "That's what we like to hear."

Robin nodded. "We knew something was wrong with the way we do our taxes now—namely that we're so inefficient at it that it's not getting us any closer to the financial goals we laid out in The Progression of Wealth Process. We just weren't sure how to go about fixing it."

"Again, that's where we come in," said Jay. "The best thing the two of you can do now is tax planning."

"That's why you're meeting with us. The reason is so that there won't be any surprises at the end of the year," Brian explained. "This is typically a good time to estimate what your taxes for the year will be so that you can make decisions to either pay estimates in or possibly start withholding less out of your pay if you expect a large refund."

"Or, if for some reason you will owe a substantial amount of tax, you can prepare yourself for its payment on April 15th," Jay added.

"Other reasons for year-end tax planning are that it assists you in deciding when income should be coming in," Brian continued. "A typical rule is to defer income, if you can, into the following year and to try to accelerate the deductions. For instance, if you bunch expenses into one year, you may be able to increase your total deductions over the adjusted gross income floor. You may also be able to gain larger deductions by paying your sales tax estimates early," he said.

"This may also be a good time to look at getting deductible interest expense in advance so that you may optimize your investment interest expenses," Jay picked up. "Remember, when it comes to tax planning, timing is everything and you should have a detailed tax projection completed by your advisor or accountant prior to the end of the year. You will often be amazed at the advantages of taking deductions early and deferring income. Also, when Robin hires employees for her business, this may become more relevant because of additional pension plan deductions, operating expenses and other business related deductions, and that sort of thing."

"Wow," said Roy, leaning back in his chair. "These are all things we never really thought about—or knew about, for that matter. Taxes have always been a sort of a muddle for us," he confessed.

"You and 200 million other people," said Jay. "It just takes time and knowledgeable advisors to sit down and figure things out with you."

"For instance, people don't realize that taxes should, at a minimum, become a twice-a-year event: once before the tax filing date of April 15th and then once again during the fall to do year-end planning. Also, whenever an event takes place, such as a sale or purchase of an investment property or changes of employment, you should consider tackling the planning right away," said Brian.

"I have here," said Jay, "the results of a little quiz I'd asked you to complete." He passed the paper over to Brian.

The Progression of Wealth Tax Checklist:

1. How do you feel about paying your taxes?

    Good___   Bad_x_

2. What tax planning strategies have you used in the past?

    a. IRAs

    b. 401(k)s

    c. Profit sharing

    d. Municipal bonds

    e. Tax advantage municipal funds

    f. Tax advantage investment strategies

    g. College savings plans

    h. Gifting to children

3. Do you feel that you are doing everything possible to legally minimize your income taxes?

    Yes_____   No_x_

After a minute, Brian slid it over to the couple, leaned over and pointed to the third item on the list. "Since you checked 'No' here, it indicates that a thorough review of your tax returns is needed," he said.

"That's what I figured," said Roy.

Robin sighed. "We certainly do need to get very serious about our tax preparation," said Robin. "Just in talking with you we've realized how important a part of our financial plan it is. The fact that we can reduce tax obligations through the years and put that money aside to be invested for better use is incentive enough."

"Not to mention the fact that the way we're doing things now just causes major headaches," added Roy.

Jay smiled. "As you get older, charitable donations may become important to you, and there are tax advantage strategies such as charitable trusts or foundations which help to not only reduce estate taxes but also offer current income tax deductions. Other things to consider are compliance with household employees, dependent parents, and the like," he said.

"I like the sound of charitable donations," said Roy. "But it's going to take some time before I completely understand what you're talking about."

Jay stood up and stretched. "It may not be as long as you think."

Chapter 9 Overview:
The Income Tax Strategy™

The Income Tax Strategy ensures that your taxes are being reduced to the lowest amount legally possible. Throughout the year your tax situation is being monitored and evaluated to ensure that you are taking advantage of every tax-deferred savings vehicle and tax deduction possible. Through tax sensitive portfolio management techniques the effects of capital gains distributions to you are minimized. The Income Tax Strategy includes the preparation of an income tax projection before the end of the year to determine if there are additional planning opportunities to lower your tax liability.

Chapter 10

CONCLUSION

"May you grow proud, dignified, and true,
and do unto others as you'd have done to you."
— R. Stewart / J. Cregan / F. Savigar

May 24th, 2003

IT WAS A BEAUTIFUL MORNING, and the Sewells were up early having breakfast.

Jack looked grumpy and half asleep. "I hate getting up this early on a Saturday. Or any day," he whined.

Robin poured a cup of coffee for her son and one for herself. "Well, it's for a good reason. It's not every day you get to see your sister speak as the valedictorian of her graduating class!"

Roy entered the kitchen carrying the camera. "This baby's got plenty of film in it. She's ready to go."

Jack slurped his coffee loudly. "I could have been valedictorian if I wanted to, too, you know."

"Right," said Roy. "Of your frat maybe."

"Alright, you two. Let's get ready to go. We don't want to be late," said Robin.

The three of them piled into the car and left for campus. They got there early enough that they were able to get decent seats towards the front of the auditorium.

As *Pomp and Circumstance* began playing over the loudspeaker, everyone stood and turned to get a better look at the graduates filing up the aisle.

"Does anyone see Morgan yet?" asked Jack, straining to look amongst the line of smiling students in caps and gowns.

"She should be at the end of the line … there she is!" said Robin excitedly. "Roy, get her attention! I want her to look this way so I can take some pictures."

"I'll get her attention," said Jack. "MO! HEY, MO!" Morgan turned her head at the sound of her brother's foghorn voice. Robin's flash went off wildly. Morgan's smile grew bigger as her mother continued snapping pictures, and her father waved his fist in the air triumphantly as she passed.

After the graduates were seated on the stage, the President of Susquehanna University introduced them, and then finally the Class Valedictorian —Morgan Sewell. As the President listed all her accomplishments, tears rolled down Robin's cheeks. She had never been prouder of her family than at that moment.

Jack broke the sentimental moment. "We should start doing the wave."

Robin turned to him and hissed furiously, "Don't you dare, young man. Don't you ruin your sister's moment to shine."

"Relax, Mom, I'm kidding," Jack grinned.

When the roar of the applause ended, Morgan began her speech:

> "I want to congratulate the class of 2003 and thank the faculty for their dedication to excellence. We came in here as young, impressionable boys and girls and we leave here as impressionable young men and women. Take a look around you. Look at the person seated to the left and right of you. These are the next leaders of our country, the next great doctors, lawyers, corporate executives, and politicians. I am honored to be a part of this class."

Morgan sneaked in a wave to her sorority sisters. A yell from the crowd of "We love you, Mo!" momentarily interrupted the tempo of her speech.

> "A lot of change has occurred during our four years here," she continued. "Terrorist attacks, the end of Saddam Hussein's reign of terror over Iraq, the fall of Enron, the dissolution of Arthur Anderson, wholesale corporate scandals, and the technology bubble. At the same time, our Nation has continued to flourish, new technology continues to be developed, new advancements in

medicine, and education continue to evolve with the times. We could not ask for a better time to go out and make our mark on the World.

"We should not take our responsibility lightly or the effects our actions have on others. What we do, what we say, how we act, and how we treat others matters. Our professors taught us about the importance of ethics and integrity and held us to a high standard. As captain of the lacrosse team I learned the value of teamwork and leadership. Admittedly, I did not understand the importance of these values at the time. But now, when I think of the world events that have taken place over the past four years, I clearly see that these values are missing in our society and in our world. So I issue a challenge to my fellow graduates: remember what you learned here, that your grades are less important than your ethics and integrity. Treat people with respect and honesty and you will be assured of leaving your mark on the world. Thank you again for this honor. Finally, I would like my family to stand up. Come on Mom, Dad and yes, even you Jack, where are you?"

"Everyone, this is my family." Morgan gestured, and the audience turned to look at the Sewells. They all applauded politely. "I can't thank them enough for the opportunities they gave me. They shaped the person who I am today and I hope I make them proud. Well graduates, let's go make our mark on the world!"

The auditorium erupted in applause and cheers and caps were flying. The President managed to calm everyone down momentarily to make his closing remarks. "Well we can all see why Morgan has chosen to further her education by pursuing her Master's and PHD in Economics. I also want to congratulate the graduates and their families and, to use Morgan's words, 'encourage you to leave your mark on the world.' But before you make that mark, Morgan whispered in my ear that there is a slight detour in that all the families are invited to the fraternity and sorority houses for graduation festivities. Go in peace and it has been a pleasure to come to know you."

"Yeah! Back to the sorority house! I knew it was a good idea to come here today!" Jack said with a grin as he high-fived Roy.

"Calm your hormones down, boys," said Robin with a smirk.

Back at the sorority house, Jack took his eyes off the girls for a minute and pulled Morgan aside. "I'm proud of you, little sister," he said with a grin.

"Thanks, Jack-o," said Morgan. "You gave me the scoop on college and got me off on the right foot. Can you believe we're both college graduates now?" she said in amazement.

"Well, everyone knew you would graduate. You were always the smart one, but I was the long shot—straight C's all the way through high school and college," said Jack.

"You made out just fine, landing a nice job after graduation," said Morgan.

"As I always said Mo, it is better to be lucky than smart," said Jack with a wink.

"Oh, enough already, Jack-o."

"Okay, okay," said Jack, "but hey, I have a graduation gift for you."

"Ooh, what is it?" she asked eagerly.

Jack handed her a large envelope. She tore open the envelope and pulled out two business cards and an account statement. "What is this?" asked Morgan in confusion.

"Dad gave this to me as a graduation gift and asked me to pass it down as a family legacy. The business cards are for Jay and Brian," said Jack.

"Mom and Dad's financial advisors?" asked Morgan.

"Yep, and now they're mine too," said Jack. "And the statement is the balance of the college savings account that Dad and Mom started for us. They were able to pay for both our colleges out of current income so Dad gave me the account and I can do what I want with it. He said since they would pay for your graduate school, I can have the college account. I am giving half of it to you. You can use it for graduate school and give Mom and Dad a break."

Morgan stared at the paper. "Is that balance right?" she asked.

"Yep," said Jack, "that's your half."

"Jack, I can't accept this! It's over $100,000!"

"There is only one catch. Before you can use it you have to meet with Jay and Brian and go through The Progression of Wealth Blueprint," said Jack.

"But I don't need an advisor yet," said Morgan.

"I thought the same thing. Trust me, they can help," said Jack.

"Aww, I love you, big bro!" said Morgan and gave Jack a big kiss. "Where did Dad and Mom go?" she asked.

"They're by the keg," said Jack. "Come on, Mo, before they embarrass you like they did to me at my graduation and start telling everyone stories about us when we were little."

"Good point," said Morgan. "Let's go act as censors."

Later that evening back at the Sewells' house Robin was still emotional from the day's events. "I can't believe our baby girl leaves for Europe in two days for the whole summer," she said, smiling.

"That was no baby girl that gave that speech," said Roy, sounding impressed.

"It sure wasn't," laughed Robin. "How did we get so lucky?"

"First Jack gets a job at Towers Perrin, the consulting firm, and now Morgan gets into Wharton. We sure did something right, didn't we?" said Roy.

"Yeah, we did a lot right," said Roy. Just then the doorbell rang. Roy came back into the living room carrying a large fruit basket.

"Who is it from?" asked Robin.

Roy read the card. "It says, 'Another milestone completed! Congratulations from Jay and Brian.' Wow. This is impressive." Roy peeked into the basket. "They even put in a box of chocolates for me."

"They're the best," smiled Robin. "It's amazing the path our lives took. I know we worked hard for what we got, but The Progression of Wealth Process took so much financial pressure off and led us to all our goals. Jay and Brian were right. The Progression of Wealth did accelerate our progress toward financial independence," she said.

"I remember how skeptical I was at first, but they kept encouraging us to continue to implement and move forward and we would see results. I am so glad I listened to you and them," said Roy. "I think the decision we made ten years ago made all the difference in the word to us financially. Now let's get started on this basket, shall we?"

From the Authors

The Sewells are a typical baby boomer family with serious financial goals. They realized that through their whole lives they had been coached and advised and were graded in everything they did except in their financial life.

Their decision to participate in The Progression of Wealth Process helped them make more money, enjoy life and achieve their goals both personal and financial. They are a typical family that has an amazing life. The only thing that stands between you and your own financial independence is a focus and commitment to a process that will lead you there. Whether it's by The Progression of Wealth Process or another financial plan, financial independence does not happen haphazardly. It must be planned for, embraced, monitored, and changed as necessary to keep you on track with your goals.

People are living longer, Americans are not saving enough, and the cost of education continues to rise. How can you expect to deal with these issues when they are upon you unless you are prepared? You must have a process that considers the risks, opportunities and strengths you have and the potential effect they have on your goals. When your financial planning process can do all this, you will be well on your way to financial independence.

So remember, every planning process starts with goals. This is the blueprint with which your financial independence should be built.

Appendices

Here we show the detailed records of the Sewells so you can see how it all fits together.

The Progression of Wealth Process™

What do you want to achieve with your wealth?™

| Roy Sewell (02 - 19 - 48) | Robin Sewell (03 - 30 - 50) |

Beyond

family legacy
grandchildren's education
down payment for kid's house
retirement at age 60

have a secure and happy life
be there for the kids
charities
help out kids and grandkids

10 Years

retirement is close
buy a boat
own a beach house
finish paying for college

provide for my parents
travel (four weeks a year)
daughter's wedding

5 Years

keep retirement on track
rent a beach house 1 month a year
cover Jack's college

family vacation (2 weeks a year)
put a pool in the yard
start my pwn business

1 Year

cover kids education
start saving more

feel secure
private high school for the kids
remodel kitchen

Date	Milestone	Amount Needed *
03-30-2010	kids, grandchildren's charity	total annual gift of $10,000
02-19-2008	financial independence	$75,000 after tax
October 2005	Morgan's wedding	$15,000
May 2003	beach house and boat	$150,000 (20% down)
June 2002	extended vacation	$3,000 per year
September 2000	Morgan's college	$20,000 (4 years)
September 1998	Jack's college	$20,000 (4 years)
June 1997	family vacation	$1,500 per year
April 1996	start business	$50,000 startup
September 1996	Morgan's High School	$7,000 (4 years)
September 1994	Jack's High School	$7,000 (4 years)
October 1994	remodel the kitchen	$15,000

* All amounts are based on prices, expenses, and costs in 1993 dollars and have not been inflated to the present year.

The Progression of Wealth Process™

Accelerating Your Progress Toward Financial Independence.

Stage I The Progression of Wealth Blueprint™

Stage II The Report Card™

The Financial Independence Cultivator™

Stage III The Investment Portfolio Optimizer™

The Cash Flow Optimizer™

Stage IV The Financial Independence Expander™

Stage V The Wealth Protector™

The Estate Planner™

The Loved Ones' Letter™

Stage VI The Income Tax Strategy™

Opportunities	Strengths	Risks
Robin's PR business	Robin's ability to make money in PR Roy's a great provider	parents' health
company stock options	ability of Robin to stay home and raise the kids	unemployment — loss of income
both good earners	Roy's a great leader and manager of people	not being there for the kids

HJ Financial Group
The Report Card™
Roy and Robin Sewell

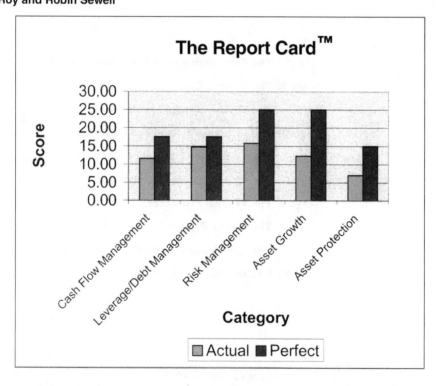

HJ Financial Group
The Report Card™

Category	Actual Score	Scoring Thresholds					Results	Comments
		A	B	C	D	F		
Cash Flow Management	Actual 11.55	Perfect 17.5	12 to 17	7 to 11	3 to 6	under 3	C	* A savings plan should be created to ensure you are maximizing your wealth accumulation ability.
Leverage/Debt Management	14.70	17.5	12 to 17	7 to 11	3 to 6	under 3	B	* Congratulations! You are using debt efficiently.
Risk Management	15.75	25	20 to 25	15 to 20	10 to 15	under 10	C	* You may be under insured in the case of a premature death. A comprehensive risk management program should be developed to ensure your family and your assets are protected.
Asset Growth	12.25	25	17 to 25	11 to 17	5 to 11	under 5	C	* An Investment Policy Statement should be developed to ensure that your asset allocation and risk level are appropriate to meet your goals.
Asset Protection	6.98	15	10 to 15	7 to 10	3 to 7	under 3	D	* Your Wills should be updated to ensure an orderly and tax efficient transfer of your wealth.

HJ Financial Group
The Report Card™

Total Composite Weight	Category	Performance Score (1-10)	Composite Score
17.50%	**Cash Flow Management**		
	Do you have sufficient cash set aside for liquidity purposes (between 2-3 months of living expenses).	9	
	Have you enough cash set aside for purchases to be made over the next 2-3 years.	8	
	Do you have access to a home equity line of credit, if necessary.	4	
	Do you have a budget/spending plan.	5	
	Do you have an annual savings plan.	5	
	Have all legal means been used to reduce taxes	5	
	Total Cash Flow Management		11.55
17.50%	**Debt Management:**		
	Is your debt/leverage ratio greater than 2:1.	9	
	Do you have access to debt on favorable terms.	9	
	Do you pay your credit card balances off monthly.	9	
	Are you prepaying your debt.	6	
	Is your debt tax-efficient.	8	
	Are you using debt as according to plan.	8	
	Total Debt Management		14.7

25.00%	**Risk Management:**	
	Do you have the appropriate amount of life insurance:	
	For Family Protection	3
	For Estate Liquidity Purposes	8
	Have you protected yourself from catastrophic loss:	
	Is your Homeowners Coverage Adequate	5
	Is your Umbrella Insurance Adequate	5
	Do you have adequate disability insurance (60-65% of current income)	8
	Do you have long-term care coverage (minimum of $150 daily benefit) or sufficient assets to self-fund.	7
	Are you business interests adequately covered:	
	Is the corporate structure appropriate	
	Has a Valuation been performed.	
	Is a buy-sell agreement in place	
	Has the buy-sell been funded for death/disability	
	or	
	How secure is your long-term future in your current position/with your current employer.	8
	Total Risk Management	15.75

25.00%   **Asset Growth**

Is your Investment Policy Statement Appropriate:

For your asset allocation	5
For your time horizon	5
For your risk tolerance	5
For your total return expectations	5

Will your current asset allocation allow you to meet your goals   5

Has risk been appropriately managed to an acceptable level.   4

How did your actual return compare with your targeted return.   5

Are your annual contributions and withdrawals appropriate according to your plan.   5

Are taxes being managed appropriately.   5

Total Asset Growth   12.25

15.00%   **Asset Protection**

Do you have a current Will   5

Are your assets appropriately titled   5

Have all beneficiaries been designated, as appropriate   4

Have you implemeted charitable giving/gifting strategies.   5

Have trusts been established and funded   4

Asset Protection   6.975

Roy and Robin Sewell

INVESTMENT POLICY STATEMENT

05/5/1994

Prepared by:
The Progression of Wealth Team
HJ Financial Group

INTRODUCTION

The purpose of this Investment Policy Statement is to establish a clear understanding between the investor Roy and Robin Sewell and the investment advisor The Progression of Wealth Team as to the investment objectives and policies applicable to the Investor's investment portfolio. This Statement will:

- establish reasonable expectations, objectives, and guidelines in the investment of the Portfolio's assets.
- set forth an investment structure detailing permitted asset classes, normal allocations and permissible ranges of exposure for the Portfolio.
- encourage effective communication between the Investor and the Advisor.
- create the framework for a well diversified asset mix that can be expected to generate acceptable long term returns at a level of risk suitable to the Investor.

The Statement has been developed from an evaluation of many key factors which impact the Investor's specific situation and investment objectives. This Statement is not a contract. It is intended to be a summary of an investment philosophy that provides guidance for the Investor and the Advisor.

THE PORTFOLIO

The Portfolio will maintain an active asset allocation strategy. The Portfolio will be invested in separate accounts and mutual funds.

The Board of Trustees of each mutual fund is ultimately responsible for selecting and monitoring investment managers to advise each fund. Investment managers are selected and monitored on the basis of the following criteria:

- the manager's specification of and adherence to a clearly articulated and appropriate investment philosophy and process.
- material changes in the manager's organization and personnel.
- comparisons of performance results to appropriate indices that take into account asset class and investment style.

Each investment manager is responsible for managing the assets of a particular mutual fund in accordance with the stated objectives and policies of that fund as set forth in each prospectus. The Investor should read this information carefully before investing.

INVESTMENT OBJECTIVES

The Portfolio seeks to provide long-term capital appreciation on an after-tax basis, with current income exempt from federal taxes as a secondary goal.

GUIDELINES AND POLICIES

Time Horizon

The Portfolio is suitable for investors with an investment horizon of five to ten years and who are seeking to minimize the impact of taxes on their investment returns. Capital values do fluctuate over shorter periods and the investor should recognize that the possibility of capital loss does exist no matter what the Investor's investment time horizon may be. However, historical asset class return data suggest that the risk of principal loss over a holding period of three years or longer can be minimized with the long-term investment mix employed by the Portfolio.

Risk Tolerances and Performance Expectations

The Investor recognizes that the objectives of the Portfolio cannot be achieved without incurring a certain amount of principal volatility. The Portfolio has an 80% commitment to global equities and a 20% allocation to global fixed income securities. The core of the Portfolio is invested in U.S. and international equity securities. The U.S. equity portion of the strategy consists primarily of an actively managed U.S. large cap component. This actively managed large cap allocation will employ tax-management strategies at several levels. The tax-managed portion of the Portfolio is augmented to actively managed small company and intermediate equity securities, including emerging markets equities. 12% of the Portfolio is invested in intermediate-term municipal fixed income securities to provide income exempt from federal taxes and further reduce the fluctuation of returns. In addition, an allocation to high yield bonds, international fixed income and emerging markets debt provide additional diversification and the potential for further return enhancement.

No guarantees can be given about future performance and this Statement shall not be construed as offering such guarantee. For illustrative purposes solely, historical results of a portfolio of assets combined in a manner consistent with the normal weightings of the Portfolio for any one, three, five and ten year periods, are provided below and on the following page.

Recommended Portfolio: Historical Annual Return

Historical Annualized Returns (After-Tax) Index Assets/Normal Weights				
	10 year	**5 year**	**3 year**	**1 year**
95th Percentile	13.4%	16.1%	18.7%	27.8%
Expected Return	8.0%	8.0%	8.0%	8.0%
5th Percentile	1.7%	-0.6%	-2.9%	-9.7%

Note: The Annualized Return History above are based on historical asset class returns using a variety of market indicators, including among others the following indicators: U.S. stocks – S&P 500 Index; Ibbotson U.S. Small Cap; Developed International stocks – MSCI EAFE Index; Emerging Markets Equity – IFC Investable Index; U.S. Bonds – U.S. Intermediate-Term Government; U.S. Short-Term Government, U.S. Long-Term Government, Lehman 3-10 Year Index, U.S. Long-Term Corporates, Mortgages – NAREIT; International Bonds – Salomon WGBI Index; High Yield Bonds – CSFB High Yield Index; Emerging Markets Debt – J.P. Morgan EMBI+; Fixed Annuities – U.S. Long-Term Corporates; Real Estate – Real Estate Composite; Cash – Ibbotson 30 Day T-Bill. Based on Historical Returns there is a 95% chance of realizing a return that is greater than the 5th percentile return. And, there is a 5% chance of exceeding the 95th percentile return. Individual asset allocation portfolios may perform better or worse than the representative asset class indicated.

These performance results do not reflect the deduction of advisory fees. Actual returns will be reduced by advisory fees and any other expenses the account may incur in the management of the account. Advisory fees are described in Part II of the Advisor's Form ADV.

Asset Allocation

Academic research suggests that the decision to allocate total account assets among various asset classes will far outweigh security selection and other decisions that impact portfolio performance. After reviewing the long-term performance and risk characteristics of various asset classes and balancing the risks and rewards of market behavior, the following asset classes were selected to achieve the objectives of the Portfolio.

To implement the recommended Asset Allocation, the Portfolio will invest in numerous mutual funds which focus on specific segments of each asset class.

Asset Class		Normal Weights
Fixed Income		19%
Equity	(U.S.)	56%
	(International)	24%
Cash		1%

Rebalancing Procedures

From time-to-time, market conditions may cause the Portfolio's investment in various mutual funds to vary from the established allocation. To remain consistent with the asset allocation guidelines established by this Statement, each mutual fund in which the Portfolio invests will be reviewed on a quarterly basis and rebalanced back to the normal weighting if the actual weighting varies by 3% or more from the recommended weighting.

DUTIES AND RESPONSIBILITIES

Investment Advisor

The Progression of Wealth Team is responsible for assisting the Investor in making an appropriate asset allocation decision based on the particular needs, objectives, and risk profile of the Investor. The Advisor will be available on a regular basis to meet with the Investor and periodically review the Portfolio for suitability based on information provided by the Investor. The Advisor should provide the Investor with the current prospectus for each mutual fund in the Portfolio selected.

Investor

Roy and Robin Sewell must provide the Advisor with all relevant information on financial condition, net worth, and risk tolerances and must notify the Advisor promptly of any changes to this information. The Investor should read and understand the information contained in the prospectus of each mutual fund in the Portfolio selected.

ADOPTION OF INVESTMENT POLICY STATEMENT

I (we) have reviewed, approved and adopted this Investment Policy Statement prepared with the assistance of The Progression of Wealth Team.

_____

Roy and Robin Sewell   **Date**

_____

The Progression of Wealth Team   **Date**
HJ Financial Group

The Progression of Wealth™
HJ Financial Group
Certified Public Accountants
Business and Personal Financial Advisors

The Loved Ones' Letter Checklist

Name: _____   SS# _____

Checklist

Section Number	Description	Date last Updated
I	General Information	_____
II	Contact Information	_____
III	Detailed Banking and Investment Account	_____
IV	Personal Property Listing	_____
V	Debts and Obligations	_____
VI	Insurance Policies	_____
VII	Employment History	_____
VIII	Summary of Employee Benefits	_____
IX	Estate Planning Documents	_____
X	Other Pertinent Information	_____
XI	Burial Wishes and Arrangements	_____

Date:_____ Initials: _____

1000 Germantown Pike, Suite H-I, Plymouth Meeting, PA 19462
610 . 272 . 4700   Fax: 610 . 272 . 6785
www.hjfinancialgroup.com

The Loved Ones' Letter Checklist Page 1

The Progression of Wealth™
HJ Financial Group
Certified Public Accountants
Business and Personal Financial Advisors

Name: _____ SS# _____

Section I. General Information

Full Name: _____

Date of Birth: _____

Other Names Used: (e.g. maiden name) _____

Marital Status: _____ single _____married _____divorced _____widow

Spouse's Name: _____ SS#: _____

Children's Information

Name	SS#	Date of Birth	Home Address

Date:_____ Initials: _____

1000 Germantown Pike, Suite H-1, Plymouth Meeting, PA 19462
610 . 272 . 4700   Fax: 610 . 272 . 6785
www.hjfinancialgroup.com

The Loved Ones' Letter Checklist Page 2

The Progression of Wealth™
HJ Financial Group
Certified Public Accountants
Business and Personal Financial Advisors

Name: _____ SS# _____

Section II. Contact Information

My Progression of Wealth Advisor is:

Advisor Name (Primary): _____

Advisor Name (Secondary): _____

Advisor's Assistant: _____

Company Name: _____

Address: _____

Work Phone: _____

Home Phone: _____

Cell Phone: _____

Fax: _____

Email Address #1: _____

Email Address #2: _____

NOTE: My Progression of Wealth Advisor handles all my financial affairs and
has a complete listing of all other specialists that are part of my Progression of Wealth team.

Date:_____ Initials: _____

1000 Germantown Pike, Suite H-I, Plymouth Meeting, PA 19462
610 . 272 . 4700   Fax: 610 . 272 . 6785
www.hjfinancialgroup.com
The Loved Ones' Letter Checklist Page 3

169

The Progression of Wealth™
HJ Financial Group
Certified Public Accountants
Business and Personal Financial Advisors

Name: _____   SS# _____

Section III. Detailed Banking and Investment Account Information
Not Supervised by My Progression of Wealth Advisor

Account Registration	Account Number	Money Manager / Custodian	Account Type

Date:_____   Initials: _____

1000 Germantown Pike, Suite H-1, Plymouth Meeting, PA 19462
610 . 272 . 4700   Fax: 610 . 272 . 6785
www.hjfinancialgroup.com
The Loved Ones' Letter Checklist Page 4

170

The Progression of Wealth™
HJ Financial Group
Certified Public Accountants
Business and Personal Financial Advisors

Name: _____   SS# _____

Section IV. Personal Property Listing

Residences and Real Estate

Property Address	Title / Ownership	Type / Description	Location of Deed

Vehicles

Make / Model / Year	Registration	VIN	Location of Title

Artwork, Jewelry, and Other Valuables

Description	Ownership	Quantity	Physical Location

Date: _____   Initials: _____

1000 Germantown Pike, Suite H-I, Plymouth Meeting, PA 19462
610 . 272 . 4700   Fax: 610 . 272 . 6785
www.hjfinancialgroup.com

The Loved Ones' Letter Checklist Page 5

The Progression of Wealth™
HJ Financial Group
Certified Public Accountants
Business and Personal Financial Advisors

Name: _____ SS# _____

Section V. Debts and Obligations

Financial and Lending Institutions

Lender	Account Number	Loan Type	Location of Note / Mortgage

Credit Cards and Open / Unused Lines of Credit

Lender	Account Number	Loan Type	Location of Note

Other Obligations and Guarantees

Lender	Primary Borrower	Purpose	Description of Collateral Assigned

Date:_____ Initials: _____

1000 Germantown Pike, Suite H-1, Plymouth Meeting, PA 19462
610 . 272 . 4700   Fax: 610 . 272 . 6785
www.hjfinancialgroup.com

The Loved Ones' Letter Checklist Page 6

The Progression of Wealth™

HJ Financial Group
Certified Public Accountants
Business and Personal Financial Advisors

Name: _____ SS# _____

Section VI. Insurance Policies
Not Supervised by My Progression of Wealth Advisor

Life Insurance

Company	Account Number	Type	Face Amount	Location of Policy

Health, Disability, and Long-Term Care Insurance

Company	Account Number	Type	Benefits / Coverages	Location of Policy

Property, Auto, Casualty, and Liability Insurance

Company	Account Number	Type	Coverages	Location of Policy

Date:_____ Initials: _____

1000 Germantown Pike, Suite H-1, Plymouth Meeting, PA 19462
610 . 272 . 4700   Fax: 610 . 272 . 6785
www.hjfinancialgroup.com

The Loved Ones' Letter Checklist Page 7

The Progression of Wealth™
HJ Financial Group
Certified Public Accountants
Business and Personal Financial Advisors

Name: _____ SS# _____

Section VII. Employment History

Please list your employment history in chronological order starting with the most recent.

Employer Name and Address	Contact Person and Phone Number	Dates of Employment	Are you entitled to any benefits?

Date:_____ Initials: _____

1000 Germantown Pike, Suite H-I, Plymouth Meeting, PA 19462
610 . 272 . 4700   Fax: 610 . 272 . 6785
www.hjfinancialgroup.com

The Loved Ones' Letter Checklist Page 8

The Progression of Wealth™

HJ Financial Group
Certified Public Accountants
Business and Personal Financial Advisors

Name: _____ SS# _____

Section VIII. Summary of Employee Benefits

Employer Name: _____

Home Office Address: _____

Phone Number:_____

Human Resource Contact: _____

Employee ID Number, if applicable: _____

Date of Hire: _____

Please check the benefits that apply.

Type of Benefit	Description / Amount
Retirement Plan	
Life Insurance	
Health Insurance	
Long-Term Care Insurance	
Disability Insurance	
Deferred Compensation	
Stock Ownership	
Stock options	
Cafeteria Plan	
Other: _____	

Date:_____ Initials: _____

1000 Germantown Pike, Suite H-1, Plymouth Meeting, PA 19462
610 . 272 . 4700   Fax: 610 . 272 . 6785
www.hjfinancialgroup.com

The Loved Ones' Letter Checklist Page 9

The Progression of Wealth™
HJ Financial Group
Certified Public Accountants
Business and Personal Financial Advisors

Name: _____   SS# _____

Section IX. Estate Planning Documents

Please complete the following chart as it relates to estate planning documents that you have executed.

Document	Location of Document	Date Signed and Executed
Will		
Living Will		
Medical Power of Attorney		
Medical Directive		
General Power of Attorney		
Living Trust		
Insurance Trust		
Charitable Trust		
Minor's Trust		
Custodial Trust		
Organ Donation		
Pre-Nuptial Agreement		
Post-Nuptial Agreement		
Divorce Decree		
Citizenship Papers		
Burial Agreement		

Date:_____   Initials: _____

The Progression of Wealth™
HJ Financial Group
Certified Public Accountants
Business and Personal Financial Advisors

Name: _____   SS# _____

_____ I have other valuables not disclosed elsewhere:

Property 1 Description: _____

Property 1 Location: _____

Property 2 Description: _____

Property 2 Location: _____

Property 3 Description: _____

Property 3 Location: _____

Property 4 Description: _____

Property 4 Location: _____

Please note any other matters of importance that you would like to have disclosed.

_____

_____

_____

_____

_____

_____

_____

_____

_____

_____

_____

_____

_____

_____

_____

Date: _____   Initials: _____

1000 Germantown Pike, Suite H-1, Plymouth Meeting, PA 19462
610 . 272 . 4700   Fax: 610 . 272 . 6785
www.hjfinancialgroup.com

The Loved Ones' Letter Checklist Page 11

177

The Progression of Wealth™

HJ Financial Group
Certified Public Accountants
Business and Personal Financial Advisors

Name: _____ SS# _____

Section X. Other Pertinent Information

Please put an "X" next to those items that apply and complete the necessary additional information as appropriate.

_____ **I have a safe deposit box.**
Location of box: _____
Location of keys and/or combination: _____
Description of contents: _____
How I would like the contents distributed: _____
_____
_____

_____ **I have a personal safe.**
Location of safe: _____
Location of keys and/or combination: _____
Description of contents: _____
How I would like the contents distributed: _____
_____
_____

_____ **I am currently a Trustee for a Trust.**
Name of Trust:_____
Person to contact regarding the Trust: _____

_____ **I am the guardian / godparent of children.**
Names of children: _____
Person to contact regarding this relationship:_____

_____ **I have the following on-line accounts that are password-protected:**

Name of Account	Account Number	User ID	Password

Date:_____ Initials: _____

1000 Germantown Pike, Suite H–1, Plymouth Meeting, PA 19462
610 . 272 . 4700   Fax: 610 . 272 . 6785
www.hjfinancialgroup.com

The Loved Ones' Letter Checklist Page 12

The Progression of Wealth™

HJ Financial Group
Certified Public Accountants
Business and Personal Financial Advisors

Name: _____   SS# _____

Section XI. Burial Wishes and Arrangements

At My Death

I ___**wish** ___**I do not wish** to have my usable organs donated.
My consent to such donation will be found on the back of my driver's license or in a document located at the following address:

_____

I ___**have** ___**I have not** provided direction with respect to artificial life support systems. If I have provided for the removal of such systems, my Living Will (or Health Care Power of Attorney) can be found at the following address:

_____

Please contact the following person immediately:
Name: _____
Address: _____
Phone: _____
Relationship: _____

If that person cannot be reached, please contact the following person:
Name: _____
Address: _____
Phone: _____
Relationship: _____

My personal physician is:
Name: _____
Address: _____
Phone: _____
Emergency: _____

I wish my remains to be delivered to:
☐ Cemetery
☐ Individual
☐ Medical Facility
Name: _____
Address: _____
Phone: _____

The funeral home I have chosen to handle the necessary arrangements is:
Name: _____
Address: _____
Phone: _____
Individual Counselor: _____

If interred, I wish my remains ☐ to be buried
☐ placed in a mausoleum

If cremated, I wish them to be disposed of as follows: _____
_____
_____

I ___**have** ___**have not** made arrangements with the funeral home along with the necessary prepayments. If I have made such arrangements, the documents may be located at:
_____
_____
_____

and more specifically in: _____
_____

Date:_____ Initials: _____

1000 Germantown Pike, Suite H-1, Plymouth Meeting, PA 19462
610 . 272 . 4700   Fax: 610 . 272 . 6785
www.hjfinancialgroup.com

The Loved Ones' Letter Checklist Page 13

The Progression of Wealth™

HJ Financial Group
Certified Public Accountants
Business and Personal Financial Advisors

Name: _____ SS# _____

I Wish The Following Arrangements:

I Wish:
☐ Visitation for _____ days
☐ To be interred immediately

I wish the service to be at the:
☐ Funeral Home
☐ Cemetery
☐ Church
☐ Synagogue
Name: _____
Address: _____
Phone: _____

I wish the following type of burial container:
Casket or urn of:
☐ Metal
☐ Wood
☐ Ceramic
☐ Material covered wood
Specific Material: _____
Specific Color: _____
For burial only:
    ☐ Protected   ☐ Unprotected
    ☐ Vault   ☐ Concrete box

I wish a ___**nonreligious** ___**a religious** Service. If a religious service, I prefer the following cleric to preside:
Name: _____
Address: _____
Phone: _____
Should the cleric not be available, I am of the _____ faith and ask
Name: _____
my (relationship)_____
to select an appropriate substitute.

I wish:
☐ A private service
☐ Open Visitation

I wish:
☐ Music
☐ No music
☐ Flowers
☐ No Flowers
Donations in lieu of flowers to the following charity:
Name: _____
Address: _____

I wish my remains to be:
☐ Viewed
☐ Not viewed
before disposition.
    If viewed, I wish a
    ☐ 1/2 couch (half opened casket)
    ☐ Full couch

I wish to be wearing the following:
_____
_____
_____

These items are located at the following address:
_____
and more specifically in:
_____

I ___**wish** ___**do not wish** a cortege.
If I have a cortege, I wish the following:
☐ A family car
☐ A flower car
☐ A lead car

I wish the following to be buried or cremated with me:
_____
_____
_____

Date:_____ Initials:_____

The Progression of Wealth™
HJ Financial Group
Certified Public Accountants
Business and Personal Financial Advisors

Name: _____ SS# _____

I wish the following to be notified regarding the funeral/visitation:

      Name   Address   Phone

1 _____
2 _____
3 _____
4 _____
5 _____
6 _____
7 _____
8 _____
9 _____
10 Fraternal Organization: _____
11 Veterans Organization: _____
12 Former Spouse: _____
13 Accountant: _____
14 Attorney: _____
15 Financial Planner: _____

I wish the following type of monument

_____

I Wish the Following Notice To Be Placed in the Following
  Publications:
Notice: (If none, state so) _____
_____
Publication: _____
Address: _____
Publication: _____
Address: _____

I wish ___**to have** ___**not to have** a memorial service at a
  date subsequent to my funeral. I wish the service to be held
  at:
Name: _____
Address: _____
Phone: _____

I would like the following epitaph

_____
_____
_____

If my funeral was not prepaid, funds are
☐ Immediately available from the following source:
Address: _____
Specific location:_____
Phone: _____

☐ If the funds to pay the cost are not immediately available,
  my personal representative is:
Name: _____
Address: _____
Phone: _____

Date:_____ Initials: _____

1000 Germantown Pike, Suite H-1, Plymouth Meeting, PA 19462
610 . 272 . 4700   Fax: 610 . 272 . 6785
www.hjfinancialgroup.com

The Loved Ones' Letter Checklist Page 15

The Business Owner's Progression of Wealth™

Stage I The Progression of Wealth Process™

Once you have completed The Progression of Wealth Process, you will have accelerated your progress toward financial independence. You will have a clear vision of your future and a plan to achieve it. In addition, you will be able to save more money, your assets will be properly allocated, structured and protected, your investment portfolio will be optimized to maximize your return and minimize your risk, you will have a comprehensive risk management and estate plan, you will have reduced your taxes, and you will never have to worry about money again. But most important, you will be making more money, enhancing your lifestyle and achieving your goals — personal and financial.

Stage II The Controllership and CFO Services™

During this stage you leave the numbers to us:

- Accounting department management
- Financial statement analysis
- Cash flow projections
- Profitability enhancement
- Payroll management
- Budget preparation and monitoring
- Financial statement - Audit Compilation or Review
- Business financial planning
- Forecasts and projections
- Human resources issues
- Negotiations with banks, leasing companies, etc.
- Employee benefits and 401k plans
- Asset management
- Strategic planning
- Accounting policies and procedures
- Accounting software maintenance and setup

STAGE III The Income Tax Strategy™

… ensures that your business and personal taxes are being reduced to the lowest amount legally possible. Throughout the year your tax situation is being monitored and evaluated to ensure that you are taking advantage of every tax-deferred savings vehicle and tax deduction possible.

The Income Tax Strategy also ensures the accurate and timely filing of your tax returns. It provides you peace of mind that your tax return was prepared and reviewed by CPAs and they will represent you if selected for an IRS Audit.

STAGE IV The Successful Plan™

During this stage we develop specific strategies for maximizing the value of your business:

- Designing shareholder agreements
- Shareholder compensation formulas
- Creating and funding buy-sell agreements
- Retirement plans and deferred compensation agreements
- Stock-option agreements
- Stock gifting strategies
- Family limited partnerships
- Design of corporate structure
- Ownership transfer answers
- Business valuation
- Business and personal estate plan

HJ Financial Group
CERTIFIED PUBLIC ACCOUNTANTS
BUSINESS AND PERSONAL FINANCIAL ADVISORS
Suite H-1, 1000 Germantown Pike
Plymouth Meeting, Pennsylvania 19462
PH: 610 ~ 272 ~ 4700 ~ FAX: 610 ~ 272 ~ 6785
www.hjfinancialgroup.com

This book was set in Adobe Minion types
by Michael Höhne
in 2003